Business Cards

Business Cards

Dynamic Graphic Design

GRAPHIC *details*

An Imprint of

PBC INTERNATIONAL, INC.

Distributor to the book trade in the United States and Canada:
Rizzoli International Publications Inc.
300 Park Avenue South
New York, NY 10010

Distributor to the art trade in the United States and Canada:
PBC International, Inc.
One School Street
Glen Cove, NY 11542
1-800-527-2826
Fax 516-676-2738

Distributor throughout the rest of the world:
Hearst Books International
1350 Avenue of the Americas
New York, NY 10019

Library of Congress Cataloging-in-Publication Data

Business cards: dynamic graphic design / by the editors of PBC
International, Inc.
    p.   cm.
    Includes index.
    ISBN 0-86636-188-X
    1. Advertising cards--Design.   I. PBC International.
    NC1002.C4B87 1993   92-35857
    741.6'85--dc20   CIP

ISBN 0-86636-239-8 (pbk)

CAVEAT—Information in this text is believed accurate, and will pose no
problem for the student or casual reader. However, the author was often
constrained by information contained in signed release forms, information
that could have been in error or not included at all. Any misinformation (or
lack of information) is the result of failure in these attestations. The author
has done whatever is possible to insure accuracy.

To assure quality reproduction, some business cards are shown at 90 percent
actual size. Others are shown significantly larger than actual size to reveal
subtle design details.

Printed in Hong Kong

Typography by
TypeLink, Inc.

10 9 8 7 6 5 4 3 2 1

Contents

Eric Baker
Principal
Eric Baker Design Associates, Inc.
New York, NY

Eric Baker is principal of Eric Baker Design Associates, Inc., a New York-based design firm. The group produces a wide range of projects in the field of publishing and corporate communications.

Mr. Baker is an active member of The American Institute of Graphic Arts and is a board member of the New York Chapter.

He is co-author of *Trademarks of the 20's & 30's* and *Trademarks of the 40's & 50's*, and author of *Great Inventions/Good Intentions: An Illustrated History of American Design Patents*. He is also acting design director of *The New Republic*.

Mr. Baker is a two-time recipient of the National Endowment for the Arts Design Grant for his independent design history projects. His work has appeared in *Print, Communication Arts, HOW, Domus, Metropolis, Blueprint, ID, The New York Art Directors Annual, British Design and Art Direction* and *GRAPHIS.*

A native of San Diego, California, Mr. Baker studied at the San Francisco Academy of Art and the California College of Arts and Crafts. He resides in Manhattan.

In an area measuring $2 \times 3\frac{1}{2}$ inches, the business card provides the designer with an opportunity to express who a client is and what they do. That's not a lot of real estate to deal with. And yet, perhaps because of the limitations of size and quantity of information, the business card is one of my favorite things to design.

In a world increasingly shaped by technology, the business card remains a very personal form of communication. It says "this is who I am and this is what I do." It is an opportunity to make a statement—to tell the recipient, in a unique way, something about yourself and your business.

Too often, designers miss a great chance to do something really exciting. Instead, they are inclined to go along with fads, using type that is too trendy, for example. A business card should last, and, therefore, the designer should take longevity into account in the overall design.

Given the size of a standard business card, scale is everything—using type that is even one point size too large will ruin an otherwise beautiful design.

And, oh yes, don't forget to check your spelling.

Michael Gericke
Senior Associate
Pentagram Design
New York, NY

A business card. It's a small piece of paper that fits in a wallet, and it's a silent introduction to the personality of its owner. It is almost always given to strangers in a ritual that has been unchanged for centuries.

My card has 12 words and 4 numbers. It's an extremely efficient form of communication—a miniaturized version of a letterhead without the letter. Designing a business card is like creating costumes for actors in the theater; the designer must shape that first impression so it has the right tone, character and ego of its owner—all on a surface measuring approximately one-fifteenth the size of this page.

The texture of the paper, the typeface, the use of color, the choice between conceptual, stylistic or corporate imagery, are all serious factors to be considered.

But ultimately it's the person, not the card, that will make the phone ring.

Michael Gericke is a Senior Associate in Pentagram's New York office where he has been responsible for identity programs, corporate communications design, packaging, and promotions for Agfa, Champion, Citibank, IBM, Neiman Marcus, the National Football League and many others. He has recently produced comprehensive identities for CBS's TV coverage of the 1992 and 1994 Olympic Games, the Hotel Hankyu International in Japan, and the FIFA World Cup soccer championships scheduled for 1994 in the United States.

Educated at the University of Wisconsin, Mr. Gericke moved to Boulder, Colorado, and spent several years at Communication Arts where he acted as design director for a multi-million dollar signage and environmental design program for the 1984 New Orleans World's Fair.

Michael Gericke has received accolades from the New York Art Directors Club, American Center for Design, and the "Most Memorable Poster in the World" exhibition in Paris. He currently serves on the executive committee of the American Institute of Graphic Arts/New York and is a frequent lecturer on design at universities and professional organizations.

Photograph © Beatriz Coll

Judi Radice

Principal
Judi Radice Design Consultant
San Francisco, CA

Judi Radice is principal of Judi Radice Design Consultant (JRDC), based in San Francisco, California. She has more than thirteen years' experience directing and producing design and packaging programs for retailers and the hospitality industry.

Educated at School of Visual Arts and Parsons School of Design in New York City, she has been a creative director, art director and production manager at major advertising agencies and corporations both in New York and San Francisco.

As vice president/creative director for The Nature Company in 1990-91, and design director for Spectrum Foods in 1987-1990, she directed complex programs including brand identity, packaging design, collateral, architectural graphics, catalog production and visual merchandising elements.

Judi Radice has authored several design books including, most recently, *The Best of Shopping Bag 2, Menu Design 5* and *Restaurant Design 3*, published by PBC International.

A business card is an image piece—it should have personality, and it should project the image that best serves the client. For example, I tend to prefer unusual formats that break away from the traditional 2 × 3½-inch standard. But if the card is for a conservative client or company, an unusual format may not be appropriate. The professionals I work for in the food, wine and entertainment industry offer greater flexibility, and I take that into account when producing their cards. The best advice is to make sure that the design conveys the style and personality of the person or company that the card will represent.

Here are some general guidelines that I follow:

Paper/stock selection
Don't skimp in this area. Business cards are held, so the paper should feel wonderful and speak of quality.

Typography/calligraphy
This choice depends on the client's needs and the overall identity design. The type for address, name and phone number should be legible; it shouldn't be a chore for the recipient to find the name or phone number.

Size/shape
If formats are too odd, they may defeat the purpose. I have seen people cut cards down to fit into uniform Rolodex or plastic sleeve holders.

Color
Less color is cost-effective, and more color doesn't always mean better. The same basic rule that applies to logo design applies here: the design must work in black and white. Color just makes it better and should be used wisely. Solid washes are unexpected and can enhance the overall presentation.

Special Features
Engraved or letterpress cards with classic typography on exquisite paper can make a wonderful business card presentation. Costs for foil stamping, embossing and die cutting vary widely depending on complexity and quantity. An intricate foil stamp in a run of 250 cards would be cost prohibitive whereas 2,500 cards with a moderately simple magnesium die foil stamping might be surprisingly affordable. I've also seen creative uses of thermography. One that comes to mind is printing in litho inks and applying a clear thermography. Finally, two-sided cards are fun.

Why not use both sides? Here is where a solid wash can create the illusion of a duplex stock.

Budget
This is always an important issue for clients. It depends on quantity, client needs and design specifications. A business card is an important investment. My advice to clients is not to skimp on paper or printing. A business card is a first and lasting impression.

Common Pitfalls
Be sure there is a clear distinction between fax and phone numbers—they are easily confused. And avoid awkward sizes that won't fit in a Rolodex or card file.

Advice to Designers
Make sure the card you are designing is useful. Don't let the design overwhelm the information. Remember, it's a calling card.

James Sebastian
President, Creative Director
Designframe, Inc.
New York, NY

There are no rules for business card design, other than the needs of the client and the image they wish to portray. In the frame of approximately $2 \times 3\frac{1}{2}$ inches, a card can introduce, remind, inform, symbolize, and entertain. The small format invites one to focus on the details as the card communicates simultaneously through hand and eye.

The choice of materials: paper, fabric, leather, metal; typography and/or calligraphy; color; and printing and finishing techniques come together in various and wonderful combinations limited only by the designer's imagination.

What constitutes good design, defies description: at one end of the spectrum is a card of simple typography, beautifully imprinted on a special paper; at the other—a design so distinctive it could be printed on almost anything with a rubber stamp.

James Sebastian holds a B.F.A. in design from the Rhode Island School of Design, as well as a B.S. in marketing. In 1976, he founded Designframe, Inc., an internationally recognized, multi-discipline marketing and communications consulting firm. Mr. Sebastian's work is included in the Museum of Modern Art Design Collection and the Library of Congress. Among the many awards won by his firm is the IDEA (Industrial Design Excellence Award) from the Industrial Designers Society of America.

Two-Sided Cards

CLIENT
First Hello
DESIGNER
John Sayles
DESIGN FIRM
Sayles Graphic Design, Inc.
MANUFACTURER
Hansen Printing
ILLUSTRATOR
John Sayles
TYPESETTER
Push-Pen, Inc.

CLIENT
San Diego Design Center
DESIGNER
Laurie Handler
John Coy
DESIGN FIRM
COY, Los Angeles
MANUFACTURER
Crown-Sojurn
TYPESETTER
Aldus Type Studio, Ltd.
DESIGN AWARDS
1986/87 *American Corporate*
Identity
1986/87 Art Directors Club of
Los Angeles

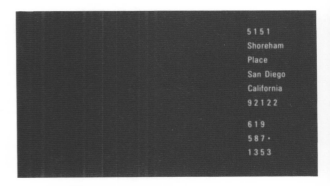

sandra higashi

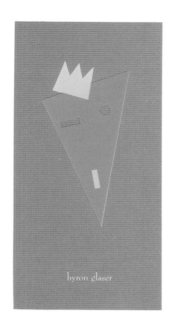

byron glaser

CLIENT
Higashi Glaser Design
DESIGNER
Byron Glaser
Sandra Higashi
DESIGN FIRM
Higashi Glaser Design

CLIENT
Todd Hauswirth
DESIGNER
Todd Hauswirth
DESIGN FIRM
C.S. Anderson Design Company
ILLUSTRATOR
Todd Hauswirth
TYPESETTER
Todd Hauswirth

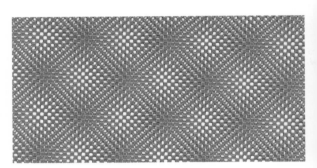

CLIENT
April Greiman, Inc.
DESIGNER
April Greiman
DESIGN FIRM
April Greiman, Inc.
MANUFACTURER
Monarch Litho

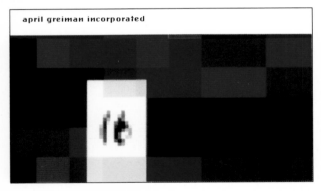

CLIENT
Peter Lord
DESIGNER
Peter Lord
TYPESETTER
Macintosh

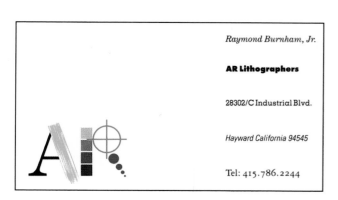

Raymond Burnham, Jr.

AR Lithographers

28302/C Industrial Blvd.

Hayward California 94545

Tel: 415.786.2244

CLIENT
AR Lithographers
DESIGNER
Earl Gee
DESIGN FIRM
Mark Anderson Design
PRINTER
AR Lithographers
ILLUSTRATOR
Earl Gee
TYPESETTER
Z Typography
DESIGN AWARDS
Art Directors Club of Los Angeles
Graphic Design:USA
DESI, Creativity
American Corporate Identity
International Logos and Trademarks
Letterheads 2/Graphic-sha (Japan)
Letterhead Collection/PIE Books (Japan)

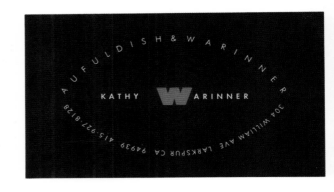

Kathy Warinner
AUFULDISH & WARINNER
graphic designers
304 william Larkspur CA 949 39
415 927·8128

bob Aufuldish
AUFULDISH & WARINNER
graphic designers
304 William Larkspur CA 94939
415 927·8128

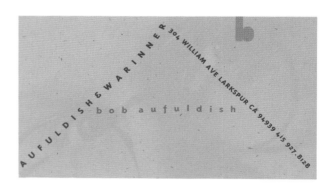

CLIENT
Aufuldish & Warinner
DESIGNER
Kathy Warinner
Bob Aufuldish
DESIGN FIRM
Aufuldish & Warinner
PRINTER
Logos Graphics
TYPESETTER
A & W

PHILIPPE SIGOUIN

président

TURQUOISE DESIGN INC.

69, RUE VAUDREUIL, HULL (QUÉBEC) J8X 2B9

(819) 771 9185 (FAX) 771 1197

CLIENT
Turquoise Design Inc.
ARTISTIC DIRECTOR
Mark Timmings
DESIGNER
Daniel Lohnes
DESIGN FIRM
Turquoise Design Inc.
MANUFACTURER
Film—Hadwen Graphics
Printing—Alcins Printing
TYPESETTER
Daniel Lohnes
PHOTOGRAPHER
Martin Lipman
DESIGN AWARDS
First Prize—*HOW* Magazine, 4th
Annual Self-Promotion Contest,
Cincinnati
1991 Gold—*Studio* Magazine
Award, Toronto
1991 Gold—Ottawa Advertising
and Sales, Ottawa
1991—AIGA Communications
Graphics Competition, New York

CLIENT
Smart Design
ART DIRECTOR
Tamara Thomsen
DESIGNER
Laura Genninger
DESIGN FIRM
Smart Design Inc.
DESIGN AWARDS
Graphis

7 WEST 18TH STREET
NEW YORK, NEW YORK 10011

TUCKER VIEMEISTER

SMART DESIGN inc.

VICE PRESIDENT DESIGN

TELEPHONE: 1 212 807 8150

FAX: 1 212 243 8514

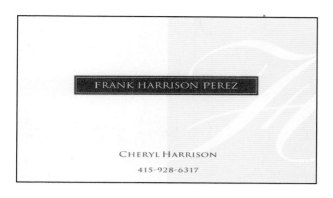

FRANK HARRISON PEREZ

CHERYL HARRISON
415-928-6317

FRANK HARRISON PEREZ

CHARLES PEREZ
415-882-9277

665 CHESTNUT STREET
SUITE THREE HUNDRED
SAN FRANCISCO CA
94133-2305

FAX: 510-271-8157
TEL: 415-474-0400

CLIENT
Frank Harrison Perez
DESIGNER
Cheryl Harrison
DESIGN FIRM
Harrison Design Group
MANUFACTURER
Western De Luna Press
TYPESETTER
Pinnacle Type

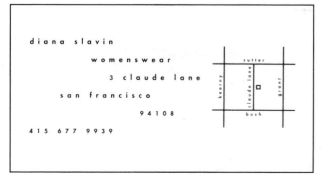

diana slavin
womenswear
3 claude lane
san francisco
94108
415 677 9939

CLIENT
Diana Slavin Womenswear
DESIGNER
Tom Bonauro
DESIGN FIRM
Tom Bonauro Design
MANUFACTURER
Logos Graphics
PHOTOGRAPHER
Paul Cruz

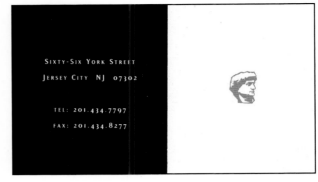

CLIENT
David Morris Design Associates
DESIGNER
Alex Bonziglia
DESIGN FIRM
David Morris Design Associates
MANUFACTURER
J.L. Printech, Inc.
TYPESETTER
Timothy O'Donnell
ILLUSTRATOR
Timothy O'Donnell

CLIENT
Z-Pix, Inc.
DESIGNER
Charles S. Anderson
Daniel Olson
DESIGN FIRM
C.S. Anderson Design Company
DESIGN AWARDS
MCAD Alumni 1992

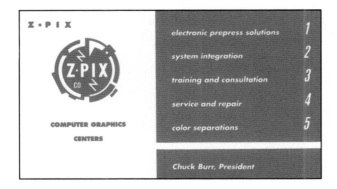

Z-PIX COMPUTER GRAPHICS CENTERS

411 2ND AVENUE NORTH

MPLS., MN 55401

PHONE (612) 371 7000

FAX (612) 371 0458

CLIENT
Pentech International, Inc.
DESIGNER
Shelley Danysh
DESIGN FIRM
Shelley Danysh Studio
MANUFACTURER
Indian Valley Printing
TYPESETTER
1P Graphics
ILLUSTRATOR
Shelley Danysh

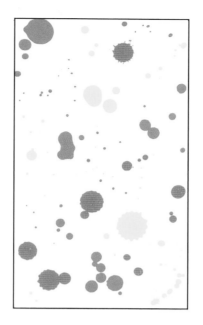

CLIENT
Final Copy
DESIGNER
Mark Oldach
DESIGN FIRM
Mark Oldach Design
PRINTER
LithoTech, Inc.
TYPESETTER
Mastertype

CLIENT
Barbara Hofling/to DESIGN
DESIGNER
Jean Mogannam
Rick Tharp
DESIGN FIRM
THARP DID IT
ILLUSTRATOR
Jean Mogannam
TYPOGRAPHER
Fotocomp

BARBARA HOFLING

to **DESIGN**

152 CORTE ANITA
GREENBRAE, CA 94904
TELEPHONE: 415.461.6705
TELEFAX: 415.461.5838

to·D or not 2·D?   3·D

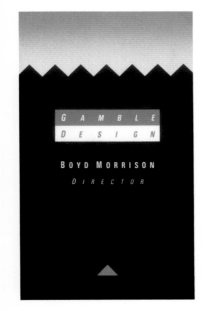

GAMBLE
DESIGN

BOYD MORRISON
DIRECTOR

Print Product &
Environmental
Graphic Design

2 & 3 DIMENSIONAL
COMMUNICATION

9 Sheafe Street
Portsmouth
New Hampshire
0 3 8 0 1

603.427.1300
☎

603.427.1320
FAX

CLIENT
Gamble Design
DESIGNER
Boyd Morrison
DESIGN FIRM
Gamble Design, Inc.
MANUFACTURER
CGC
ILLUSTRATOR
Boyd Morrison

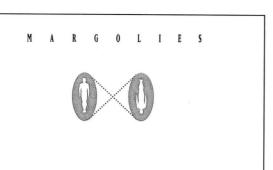

Paul Margolies
Photography
50 Harbor Oak Drive # 11
Tiburon, CA 94920
TEL. 415.621.3306
FAX 415.435.6476

CLIENT
Paul Margolies
DESIGNER
Doug Akagi
DESIGN FIRM
Akagi Design

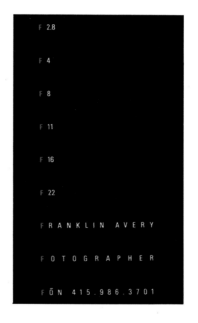

CLIENT
Franklin Avery Fotographer
DESIGNER
Kim Tomlinson
Rick Tharp
DESIGN FIRM
THARP DID IT
PRINTER
Bayshore Press
PHOTOGRAPHER
Rick Tharp
TYPOGRAPHER
FotoComp
DESIGN AWARDS
West Coast Show, *GRAPHIS*
Letterheads
Simpson Printed Paper Competition

CLIENT
Sayles Graphic Design
DESIGNER
John Sayles
DESIGN FIRM
Sayles Graphic Design, Inc.
MANUFACTURER
Acme Printing Co.
ILLUSTRATOR
John Sayles
TYPESETTER
Push-Pen, Inc.

CLIENT
Buena Vista College
DESIGNER
John Sayles
DESIGN FIRM
Sayles Graphic Design, Inc.
MANUFACTURER
Acme Printing Co.
ILLUSTRATOR
John Sayles
TYPESETTER
Printing Station

PHOTOGRAPHY
CHARLIE DANIELS

CLIENT
Charlie Daniels
DESIGNER
Lorna Stovall
DESIGN FIRM
Lorna Stovall Design
PRINTER
Printers Unlimited

ЯHqAЯ⅁OTOHq
905 NORTH COLE AVENUE
SUITE 2120
HOLLYWOOD, CA 90038
213·461·8659 FAX: 213·462·7116

MARRONE BROS., INC.
GENERAL CONTRACTORS
POST OFFICE BOX FC
LOS GATOS, CA 95031
500 E. McGLINCEY LANE
CAMPBELL, CA 95008
GREG MARRONE
408.371.4003

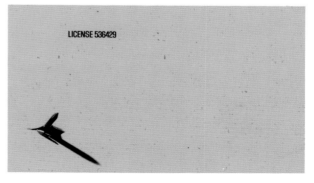

LICENSE 536429

CLIENT
Marrone Brothers, Inc.
DESIGNER
Rick Tharp
DESIGN FIRM
THARP DID IT
PHOTOGRAPHER
Dave Monley
TYPESETTER
FotoComp

CLIENT
Big H Productions
DESIGNER
Bob Aufuldish
DESIGN FIRM
Aufuldish & Warinner
PRINTER
Logos Graphics
TYPESETTER
A & W

CLIENT
Print Craft, Inc.
DESIGNER
Charles S. Anderson
Daniel Olson
DESIGN FIRM
C.S. Anderson Design Company
DESIGN AWARDS
ID Magazine 1991
Communication Arts 1990

JEANNIE ANTES
Ō KŌŌ RÄŃ BOX 2823
40780 BIG BEAR BLVD
BIG BEAR LAKE CA 92315
TELE ■ 714 ■ 866 ■ 6652

CLIENT
O KŌO RÄN CLOTHING
DESIGNER
Alan Disparte
DESIGN FIRM
Alan Disparte Design

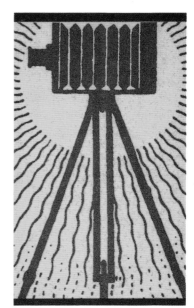

DAVID BLOMQUIST
PHOTOGRAPHY
49 PLEASANT STREET
EPPING NH 03042
[603] 679 - 2989

CLIENT
David Blomquist Photography
DESIGNER
Marc English
DESIGN FIRM
Marc English Design
MANUFACTURER
BHF Printing

CLIENT
Vertical Designs
DESIGNER
Tony Ross
DESIGN FIRM
Ross Design Inc.
ILLUSTRATOR
Tony Ross
TYPESETTER
Macintosh

VERTICAL DESIGNS INC.

•

VERTICAL BLINDS
MICRO & MINI BLINDS
PLEATED & DUETTE SHADES
SPECIALTY SHADES
LAMBERQUINS

•

JOY CAPANO

•

220 ASTRO SHOPPING CENTER
KIRKWOOD HIGHWAY
NEWARK, DE 19711
302-737-7300

REHOBOTH BEACH, DE
302-226-0680

Say:
Raa-
Dee-
Chay

CLIENT
Judi Radice Design Consultant
DESIGNER
Lance Anderson
DESIGN FIRM
Lance Anderson Design

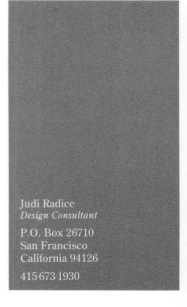

Judi Radice
Design Consultant

P.O. Box 26710
San Francisco
California 94126

415·673·1930

CLIENT
Gallery Unknown
DESIGNER
C. Alexander Cohen
DESIGN FIRM
Identity Design
MANUFACTURER
Daily Printing
TYPESETTER
Camera Ready
ILLUSTRATOR
C. Alexander Cohen

CLIENT
Cafe Lulu
DESIGNER
Patrice Eilts
DESIGN FIRM
Eilts, Anderson & Tracy Design
MANUFACTURER
Ashcray Printing, Inc.
TYPESETTER
Patrice Eilts
ILLUSTRATOR
Patrice Eilts
DESIGN AWARDS
Studio Design Awards
Letterhead & Logo Design
Three Golds—local Addy Awards

Design &
Illustration

CLIENT
**Ann Haskel Professional Weight
Training For Women**
DESIGNER
Lisa Fingerhut
DESIGN FIRM
Michael Stanard, Incorporated

CLIENT
Ray Honda
DESIGNER
Ray Honda
DESIGN FIRM
DMZ

CLIENT
The Design Company
DESIGNER
Marcia Romanuck
DESIGN FIRM
The Design Company
MANUFACTURER
Color Marketing Concepts
ILLUSTRATOR
Marcia Romanuck
DESIGN AWARDS
**The Design Show—Boston 1986
Merit Award**

CLIENT
Lisa, hairdresser
DESIGNER
Richard Hagen
DESIGN FIRM
Hula Lei
TYPESETTER
Richard Hagen
ILLUSTRATOR
Richard Hagen

CLIENT
Jacek Przybyszewski
DESIGNER
Jacek Przybyszewski
DESIGN FIRM
Jacek Przybyszewski
MANUFACTURER
Belleville Offset (Paris)
ILLUSTRATOR
Jacek Przybyszewski
TYPESETTER
Claire-Aline Bruni

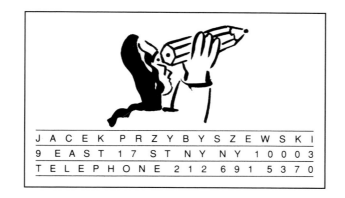

CLIENT
La Pêche
DESIGNER
Walter McCord
DESIGN FIRM
Walter McCord Graphic Design
MANUFACTURER
Lipps National Corporation
ILLUSTRATOR
Walter McCord
TYPESETTER
Derby City Litho

CLIENT
Andrea Cutler
DESIGNER
Andrea Cutler
DESIGN FIRM
A. Cutler Design
ILLUSTRATOR
Andrea Cutler
TYPESETTER
L & B N.Y.C.

CLIENT
Jack Tom Design
DESIGNER
Jack Tom
DESIGN FIRM
Jack Tom Design
ILLUSTRATOR
Jack Tom
DESIGN AWARDS
GRAPHIS Letterhead 1
GRAPHIS Logo 1
GRAPHIS Design 90
Print's Best Logos & Symbols
Creativity 21
PIE *Business Card Graphics 2*

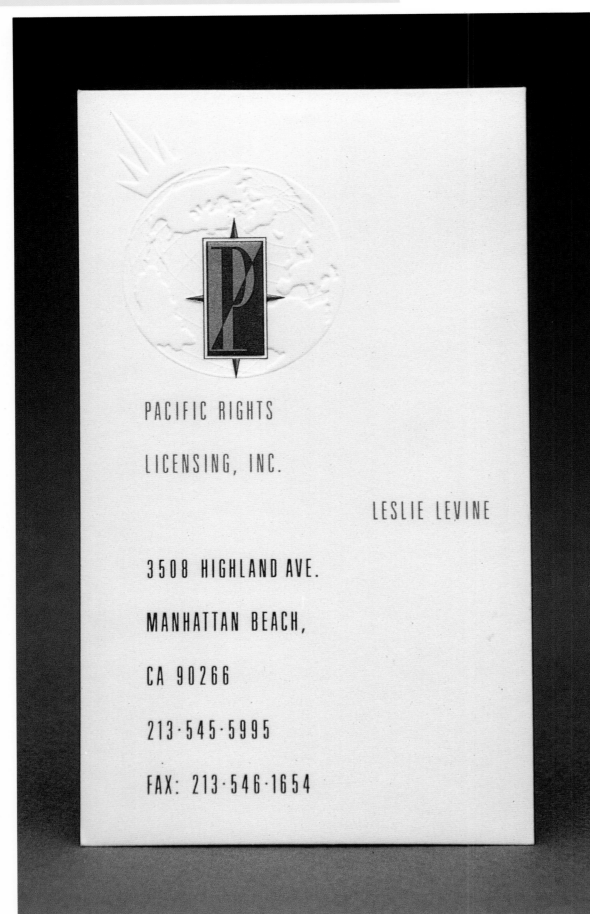

PACIFIC RIGHTS

LICENSING, INC.

LESLIE LEVINE

3508 HIGHLAND AVE.

MANHATTAN BEACH,

CA 90266

213·545·5995

FAX: 213·546·1654

CLIENT
Pacific Rights Licensing, Inc.
DESIGNER
Robert Louey
Regina Rubino
DESIGN FIRM
Louey/Rubino Design Group
PRINTER
Colour Craft Printing
TYPESETTER
Composition Type
ILLUSTRATOR
Robert Louey
Carol Martinez
DESIGN AWARDS
Graphic Design:USA
1991 DESI Awards Excellence in
Graphic Design

CLIENT
Jim Coon, Photography &
Illustration
DESIGNER
Jeff and Adrienne Pollard
DESIGN FIRM
Pollard Design
PRINTER
Warwick Press (letterpress)

CLIENT
Thrasher Graphics
DESIGNER
Jeff and Adrienne Pollard
DESIGN FIRM
Pollard Design
PRINTER
Jane Roberts (letterpress)

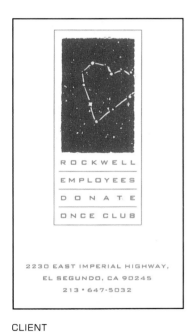

CLIENT
"Donate Once Club"
Rockwell International Corporation
DESIGNER
Robert Louey
Regina Rubino
DESIGN FIRM
Louey/Rubino Design Group
PRINTER
Rockwell Data Services Center
TYPESETTER
Composition Type
ILLUSTRATOR
Robert Louey

CLIENT
Airplay Music
DESIGNER
Adrienne Pollard
DESIGN FIRM
Pollard Design
MANUFACTURER
Allied Printing Services

TODD WARE

MASSAGE

649-1568

TODD WARE

ATHLETIC MASSAGE

SKIN & CELLULITE TREATMENTS

SWEDISH MASSAGE

JIN SHIN DO / ACCUPRESSURE

MUSCULAR REEDUCATION

REGENESIS / BIOENERGETICS

HOME
649-1568

PHONE MAIL
1-468-6273

CLIENT
Todd Ware Massage
DESIGNER
Don Weller
DESIGN FIRM
The Weller Institute for the Cure of Design, Inc.
ILLUSTRATOR
Don Weller
TYPESETTER
Chikako Weller

CLIENT
The Dandy Candy Man
DESIGNER
Rick Tharp
DESIGN FIRM
THARP DID IT
PRINTER
The Printing Post
ILLUSTRATOR
Kim Tomlinson
TYPESETTER
FotoComp
DESIGN AWARDS
The West Coast Show

KELLY O'CONNOR
HEAD CANDY MAN

THE DANDY CANDY MAN

Purveyor of Condommints

POST OFFICE BOX 2151
LOS GATOS, CA 95031
PHONE · 408.378.5600
TELEFAX · 408.354.1450

CLIENT
The Weller Institute for the Cure of Design, Inc.
DESIGNER
Don Weller
DESIGN FIRM
The Weller Institute for the Cure of Design, Inc.
ILLUSTRATOR
Don Weller
TYPESETTER
Chikako Weller

The
Weller
Institute
For
The
Cure
Of
Design,
Inc.

Cha Cha
Weller

3091
Fawn
Drive
P O Box
726
Park
City,
Utah
84060
(801)
649-9859
Fax
(801)
649-4196

Fleurs du Jour
2525 Main Street
Santa Monica, California 90405
213-399-9131

Joan Child
Owner

CLIENT
Fleurs du Jour
DESIGNER
Robert Louey
Regina Rubino
DESIGN FIRM
Louey/Rubino Design Group
PRINTER
Main Street Printing
TYPESETTER
Typographic Services
ILLUSTRATOR
Robert Louey
DESIGN AWARDS
Graphic Design:USA
1990 DESI Award—Excellence in
Graphic Design
Washington Trademark Design
International Logos & Trademarks
of the 1980's—Certificate of
Excellence

Michele Youell

Takota Traders
P.O. Box 680772
Park City, UT. 84068
801-649-0846

CLIENT
Takota Traders
DESIGNER
Don Weller
DESIGN FIRM
The Weller Institute for the
Cure of Design, Inc.
ILLUSTRATOR
Don Weller
TYPESETTER
Chikako Weller

CLIENT
Albuquerque Rape Crisis Center
DESIGNER
Gary Cascio
Steve Wedeen
DESIGN FIRM
Vaughn/Wedeen Creative
PRINTER
Albuquerque Printing
ILLUSTRATOR
Gary Cascio

Albuquerque **Rape** Crisis Center

Ginger McGirk
Crisis Services Specialist

1025 Hermosa SE
Albuquerque
New Mexico 87108
505·266·7711

University of New Mexico Mental Health Center
A United Way Agency

CLIENT
Robin Ghelerter
DESIGNER
Robin Ghelerter
DESIGN FIRM
**Robin Ghelerter Illustration &
Design**
ILLUSTRATOR
Robin Ghelerter

CLIENT
Zuma Film
ART DIRECTOR
Larry Vigon
DEISGNERS
Larry Vigon
Brian Jackson
DESIGN FIRM
Larry Vigon Studio
MANUFACTURER
Capital Press
ILLUSTRATOR
Larry Vigon

CLIENT
Spirit Films
DESIGNER
Robert Louey
Regina Rubino
DESIGN FIRM
Louey/Rubino Design Group
PRINTER
Main Street Printing
TYPESETTER
Composition Type
ILLUSTRATOR
Robert Louey
DESIGN AWARDS
Graphic Design:USA
**1990 DESI Awards—Excellence in
Graphic Design**

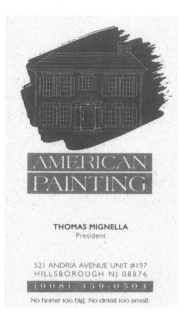

THOMAS MIGNELLA
President

521 ANDRIA AVENUE UNIT #197
HILLSBOROUGH NJ 08876
(908) 359-0503
No home too big. No detail too small.

CLIENT
THARP DID IT
DESIGNER
Rick Tharp
Karen Nomura
Jean Mogannam
Jan Heer
DESIGN FIRM
THARP DID IT
PRINTER
Simon Printing
PAPER
Simpson Starwhite Vicksburg
TYPESETTER
Frank's Type

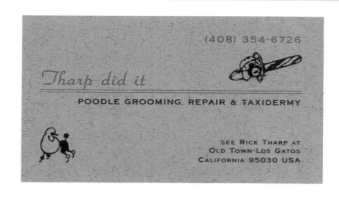

CLIENT
American Painting
DESIGNER
Jack C. Rizzo
DESIGN FIRM
Jack Rizzo Computer Aided Design
TYPESETTER
Jack Rizzo Computer Aided Design

CLIENT
Nanci Fragassi
DESIGNER
Nanci Fragassi
DESIGN FIRM
ART F X
ILLUSTRATOR
Nanci Fragassi
PHOTOGRAPHER
Advance Reproductions

CLIENT
Ken Fischer
DESIGNER
Jean Mogannam
Rick Tharp
DESIGN FIRM
THARP DID IT
PRINTER
The Prospect Press
PAPER
Simpson Starwhite Vicksburg
TYPESETTER
Graphic ArtsWest

Ellen J. Coniglio
President

28 WEST 25 TH ST.
5 TH FL. NEW YORK
NEW YORK 10010
212-243-0150 VOICE
924-2046 MODEM
924-1941 FAX

CLIENT
Gorilla Graphic Services
DESIGNER
Sean Grey
DESIGN FIRM
Sean Michael Edwards Design, Inc.
PRINTER
Helios Elberon
ILLUSTRATOR
Sandra Goijberg

CLIENT
Chicago Dog and Deli
DESIGNER
John Sayles
DESIGN FIRM
Sayles Graphic Design, Inc.
MANUFACTURER
Acme Printing Co.
ILLUSTRATOR
John Sayles
TYPESETTER
Push-Pen, Inc.

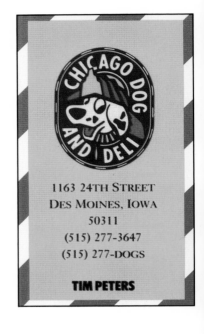

1163 24TH STREET
DES MOINES, IOWA
50311
(515) 277-3647
(515) 277-DOGS

TIM PETERS

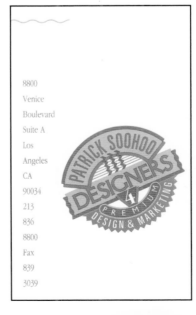

8800
Venice
Boulevard
Suite A
Los
Angeles
CA
90034
213
836
8800
Fax
839
3039

CLIENT
Patrick Soohoo Designers
DESIGNER
Patrick Soohoo
Paula Yamasaki-Ison
DESIGN FIRM
Patrick Soohoo Designers
ILLUSTRATOR
Phillip Komai
TYPESETTER
Alpha-Graphix

CLIENT
Nacho Mamma's
DESIGNER
John Sayles
DESIGN FIRM
Sayles Graphic Design, Inc.
MANUFACTURER
ABC Sign & Display
ILLUSTRATOR
John Sayles
TYPESETTER
Printing Station

CLIENT
Doobee's Donuts & Deli
DESIGNER
Robert C. Downing
DESIGN FIRM
Downing & Filzow/Graphic Design
PRINTER
Girl Friday Services, Inc.
TYPESETTER
Downing & Filzow
ILLUSTRATOR
Robert C. Downing
Nick Filzow

GIL CAMPOS

61 EAST MAIN STREET ■ NORTON, MA 02766 ■ (508) 285-2220

Bob Palumbo

91 Jackson Street

South River, NJ 08882

908/238-1080

CLIENT
The Brooklyn Bakery
DESIGNER
Yasemin K. Cullinare
DESIGN FIRM
Cullinare Design Inc.

CLIENT
Russell French Studio
DESIGNER
Dan Howard
DESIGN FIRM
Designsense
MANUFACTURER
Impressive Printing
DESIGN AWARDS
1992 Broderson Silver Award

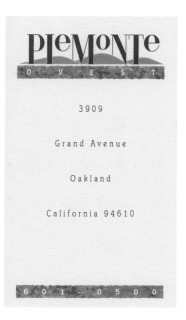

3909

Grand Avenue

Oakland

California 94610

601-0500

CLIENT
Piemonte Ovest Restaurant
DESIGNER
Cary Michael Trout
DESIGN FIRM
Trout & Trout
TYPESETTER
Macintosh/Andresen Typographics
ILLUSTRATOR
Cary Trout

Tom Duffy

1205 Burlingame Ave

Burlingame, CA 94010

415-375-1070

CLIENT
La Piñata
DESIGNER
Bruce Yelaska
DESIGN FIRM
Bruce Yelaska Design
MANUFACTURER
Vision Printing
TYPESETTER
CityType

Jeanette Koelbl
Director of Marketing

209 E. Joppa Road
Towson, Maryland 21204
301-252-1555
Fax: 301-252-9043

CLIENT
Très Bon
DESIGNER
Susan Tyrrell
DESIGN FIRM
Ruby Shoes Studio
DESIGN AWARDS
Strathmore Certificate of Excellence

KATHLEEN SPADARO
PRESIDENT

· UNLIMITED PASTABILITIES
AT A&S PLAZA
901 AVENUE OF THE AMERICAS
BOX #215 · 7th FLOOR
NEW YORK CITY 10001
212 · 629 · 9393

CLIENT
Unlimited Pastabilities
DESIGNER
Robert Louey
Regina Rubino
DESIGN FIRM
Louey/Rubino Design Group
PRINTER
Colour Craft Printing
TYPESETTER
Composition Type
ILLUSTRATOR
Robert Louey
DESIGN AWARDS
American Corporate Identity 17—
Excellence In Design

CLIENT
Nonni's Biscotti
DESIGNER
Bruce Yelaska
DESIGN FIRM
Bruce Yelaska Design
MANUFACTURER
Vision Printing
TYPESETTER
CityType
DESIGN AWARDS
Print's Regional Design Annual
American Corp. Identity
Business Card Graphics (PIE
Books)

CLIENT
Iowa Health Research Institute
DESIGNER
John Sayles
DESIGN FIRM
Sayles Graphic Design, Inc.
ILLUSTRATOR
John Sayles
TYPESETTER
Printing Station

CLIENT
Design Matters
DESIGNER
Stephen M. McAllister
DESIGN FIRM
Design Matters
MANUFACTURER
Panorama Press
TYPESETTER
Design Matters

CLIENT
Da Vinci Groep
DESIGNER
Hans Meiboom
DESIGN FIRM
Samenwerkende Ontwerpers
MANUFACTURER
Drukkerij Elco
ILLUSTRATOR
Hans Meiboom
Leonardo Da Vinci
TYPESETTER
Drukkerij Elco

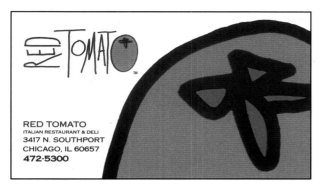

RED TOMATO
ITALIAN RESTAURANT & DELI
3417 N. SOUTHPORT
CHICAGO, IL 60657
472-5300

CLIENT
Red Tomato Inc.
Joe DiVenere
DESIGNER
Joanne & Ed Rebek
DESIGN FIRM
JOED Design

CLIENT
Tulip Films, Inc.
DESIGNER
Ivan Chermayeff
© Jonathan David
DESIGN FIRM
Chermayeff & Geismar Inc.
PRINTER
Artanis

Tulip Films, Inc.
Penthouse
145 Sixth Avenue
New York, N.Y.
10013
Tel: 212.366.5096
Fax: 212.645.6232

Jonathan David

CLIENT
Barbara Corday
ART DIRECTOR
Larry Vigon
DESIGNERS
Larry Vigon
Brian Jackson
DESIGN FIRM
Larry Vigon
ILLUSTRATOR
ANATOLY

CAN'T SING CAN'T DANCE
PRODUCTIONS

BARBARA CORDAY
PRESIDENT

300 SOUTH LORIMAR PLAZA·BUILDING 137·ROOM 2112
BURBANK, CALIFORNIA 91505

Charles Maguire
Plant Manager

SAWDUST
PENCIL CO.

44 National Road
Edison, New Jersey 08817
908·248·9088 Fax 908·248·9425

CLIENT
Sawdust Pencil Co.
DESIGNER
Shelley Danysh
DESIGN FIRM
Pentech International, Inc.
MANUFACTURER
Veitch Printing
TYPESETTER
Elizabeth Typesetting Co.
ILLUSTRATOR
Shelley Danysh
DESIGN AWARDS
1992 *American Corporate
Identity 8*
Art Directors Club of New Jersey
Merit Award

CLIENT
Frank Renlie
DESIGNER
Frank Renlie
DESIGN FIRM
Frank Renlie
MANUFACTURER
Barry Russel Printing
ILLUSTRATOR
Frank Renlie
TYPESETTER
Typecrafters

CLIENT
Cary Trout Design and Illustration
DESIGNER
Cary Michael Trout
DESIGN FIRM
Trout & Trout
TYPESETTER
Macintosh/Andresen Typographics
ILLUSTRATOR
Cary Trout

CLIENT
Keller In Print
DESIGNER
David W. Keller
DESIGN FIRM
Keller In Print
PRINTER
McClearie
TYPESETTER
Edelman Typesetting
ILLUSTRATOR
David W. Keller

CLIENT
Yellowbrick Films
DESIGNER
J. Drew Hodges
DESIGN FIRM
Spot Design

Henry Honda
Automotive Service

Automatic Transmission
Carburetors-Tune Up
Brakes-Motor Rebuilding

976 Boynton Avenue
San Jose, Calif. 95117

408 243-6508

Henry Honda Sr.

CLIENT
Henry Honda, Automotive Service
DESIGNER
Ray Honda
DESIGN FIRM
DMZ

PAM KOOPMAN

34 WEST 38TH STREET
NEW YORK, N.Y. 10018
212.768.7180
FAX 212.768.7289

CLIENT
ULURU
DESIGNER
Cheryl Harrison
DESIGN FIRM
Harrison Design Group
TYPESETTER
Pinnacle Type

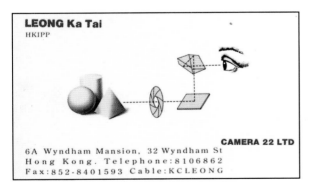

LEONG Ka Tai
HKIPP

CAMERA 22 LTD

6A Wyndham Mansion, 32 Wyndham St
Hong Kong. Telephone:8106862
Fax:852-8401593 Cable:KCLEONG

CLIENT
Camera 22 Ltd.
CREATIVE DIRECTOR
Kan Tai-keung
DESIGNER
Lau Siu Hong, Freeman
DESIGN FIRM
Kan Tai-keung Design & Associates
Ltd.

Kenneth R Deardoff

INFORMATION GRAPHICS
257 West 21st Street
New York City, N Y 10011

(212) 924-6393

CLIENT
Information Graphics
DESIGNER
Kenneth R. Deardoff
DESIGN FIRM
Information Graphics
ILLUSTRATOR
Kenneth R. Deardoff

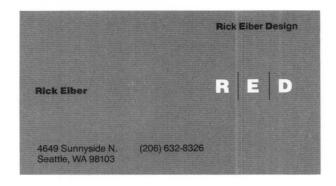

CLIENT
Rick Eiber Design (RED)
DESIGNER
Rick Eiber
DESIGN FIRM
Rick Eiber Design (RED)
MANUFACTURER
Artcraft Printing Co.
PHOTOGRAPHER
Rick Eiber
TYPESETTER
The Type Gallery

CLIENT
Sagoma Design Group
DESIGNER
Karen Gelardi
DESIGN FIRM
Sagoma Design Group
MANUFACTURER
Dale Rand Printing
ILLUSTRATOR
Karen Gelardi

CLIENT
Coblyn Design
DESIGNER
Chip Coblyn
Pam Coblyn
DESIGN FIRM
Coblyn Design
MANUFACTURER
Cobyln Design
ILLUSTRATOR
Michaelangelo
TYPESETTER
Washingtype, Inc.
DESIGN AWARDS
Art Directors Club of Metropolitan
Washington 1992
Best of Corporate Stationary

CLIENT
Aufuldish & Warinner
DESIGNER
Kathy Warinner
Bob Aufuldish
DESIGN FIRM
Aufuldish & Warinner
PRINTER
Logos Graphics
TYPESETTER
A & W

CLIENT
Kenn Tompos
DESIGNER
Kenn Tompos
DESIGN FIRM
Straight Face Studio

CLIENT
Under One Roof
DESIGNER
Alan Disparte
DESIGN FIRM
Alan Disparte Design
MANUFACTURER
Printers Unlimited
TYPESETTER
Downtown Type

CLIENT
Telephone Bar and Grill
DESIGNER
Roxanne Slimak
DESIGN FIRM
The Pushpin Group, Inc.
DESIGN AWARDS
American Corporate Identity 5

CLIENT
Deitrich's
DESIGNER
Walter McCord
DESIGN FIRM
Walter McCord Graphic Design
MANUFACTURER
Lipps National Corporation
ILLUSTRATOR
Charles Loupot
TYPESETTER
Derby City Litho
DESIGN AWARDS
Print
Menu Design
PIAS Best of Category

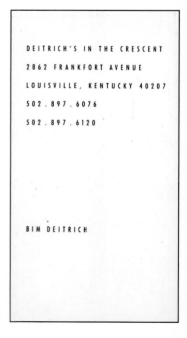

CLIENT
Rose Hairdressing For Ladies &
Gentlemen
DESIGNER
Lisa Fingerhut
DESIGN FIRM
Michael Stanard, Incorporated

CLIENT
Marie Sterte
DESIGNER
Marie Sterte
ILLUSTRATOR
Marie Sterte
TYPESETTER
Letraset

Marie Sterte

Skårdalsliden I

445 36 Bohus

tel. 031- 98 37 31

grafisk form & illustration

LA LUNA MIDWIFERY
MARGARET LOVE L.M.

P. O. BOX 725 TESUQUE, NM 87574
(505) 984-8270

CLIENT
La Luna Midwifery
DESIGNER
Patricia Curtan
DESIGN FIRM
Patricia Curtan Design & Printing

CLIENT
Théâtre du funambule
ARTISTIC DIRECTOR
Mark Timmings
DESIGNER
Daniel Lohnes
DESIGN FIRM
Turquoise Design Inc.
PRINTER
Alcins Printing
ILLUSTRATOR
Daniel Lohnes
TYPESETTER
Daniel Lohnes

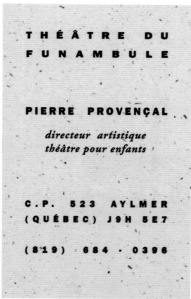

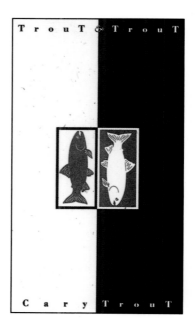

CLIENT
Trout & Trout
DESIGNER
Cary Michael Trout
DESIGN FIRM
Trout & Trout
TYPESETTER
Macintosh/Andresen Typographics
ILLUSTRATOR
Cary Trout

609 Burnett Avenue #14

San Francisco

California 94131

phone 415~282~4887

fax 415~282~4997

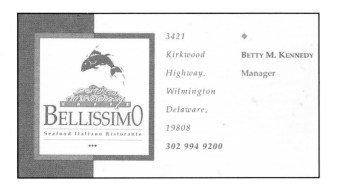

CLIENT
Caffe Bellissimo
Tim Johnson
DESIGNER
Jennifer Walker
Tony Ross
DESIGN FIRM
Ross Design Inc.
ILLUSTRATOR
June Sidwell
TYPESETTER
Macintosh
DESIGN AWARDS
Addy Award of Delaware

CLIENT
Davidé Fur
DESIGNER
Robert Louey
Regina Rubino
DESIGN FIRM
Louey/Rubino Design Group
PRINTER
Main Street Printing
TYPESETTER
Composition Type
ILLUSTRATOR
Robert Louey
DESIGN AWARDS
American Corporate Identity 16—
Excellence In Design
The Type Directors Club Certificate
of Typographic Excellence

CLIENT
Ray Honda
DESIGNER
Ray Honda
DESIGN FIRM
DMZ

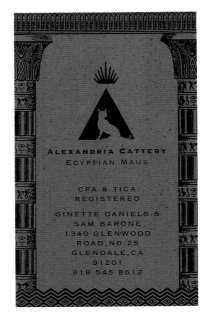

CLIENT
Alexandria Cattery
DESIGNER
Robert Louey
Regina Rubino
DESIGN FIRM
Louey/Rubino Design Group
PRINTER
Main Street Printing
TYPESETTER
Composition Type
ILLUSTRATOR
Robert Louey

CLIENT
Design Farm
DESIGN
U.G. Sato
DESIGN FIRM
Design Farm Inc.
MANUFACTURER
Yoshioka Printing Co., Ltd.
ILLUSTRATOR
U.G. Sato

CLIENT
Jack Lowry Design
DESIGNER
Jack Lowry
DESIGN FIRM
Jack Lowry Design
MANUFACTURER
Interprint, Inc.
ILLUSTRATOR
Jack Lowry
TYPESETTER
Grafix Productions

CLIENT
The Hua Shop
CREATIVE DIRECTOR
Kan Tai-keung
DESIGNER
Wong On Ming, Barry
DESIGN FIRM
Kan Tai-keung Design & Associates Ltd.

CLIENT
Family and Cosmetic Dentistry Dr. Day
DESIGNER
Dan Flynn
DESIGN FIRM
Flynn Graphic Design
TYPESETTER
Typesavers
PHOTOGRAPHER
Dan Flynn Michael Barley

CLIENT
Russell French Studio
DESIGNER
Dan Howard
DESIGN FIRM
Designsense
MANUFACTURER
Impressive Printing
DESIGN AWARDS
Broderson Award—Silver 1992

CLIENT
Wong Wai-man, Winnie
CREATIVE DIRECTOR
Kan Tai-keung
DESIGNER
Lau Siu Hong, Freeman
DESIGN FIRM
Kan Tai-keung Design & Associates Ltd.

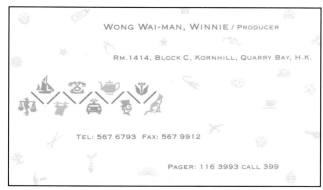

CLIENT
Mallscapes
DESIGNER
Bob Dennard
Ken Koester
DESIGN FIRM
Dennard Creative, Inc.
MANUFACTURER
Berlin Printing
ILLUSTRATOR
Ken Koester
TYPESETTER
Southwestern Typographics
DESIGN AWARDS
New York AD'66
Print's Regional Design Annual

CLIENT
Studio Allsorts
DESIGNER
Keith Martin
Dale Simonson
Dennis Nagy
Jil Weaving
DESIGN FIRM
Studio Allsorts

CLIENT
Dancing Desert Press
ART DIRECTOR
Rick Vaughn
DESIGNER
Rick Vaughn
DESIGN FIRM
Vaughn/Wedeen Creative
PRINTER
Albuquerque Printing
ILLUSTRATOR
Rick Vaughn
DESIGN AWARDS
Print's Regional Design Annual 1991
Local Addy Award

CLIENT
Cumberland Gap Productions
DESIGNER
Walter McCord
DESIGN FIRM
Walter McCord Graphic Design
MANUFACTURER
Hammond Printing
ILLUSTRATOR
George Caleb Bingham
TYPESETTER
Harlan Typographic

CUMBERLAND GAP
PRODUCTIONS

ELEANOR BINGHAM MILLER

635 WEST MAIN STREET

THIRD FLOOR

LOUISVILLE, KENTUCKY 40202

(502) 587-7348

THE FLOWER COMPANY

DAVID A. ROSSO

BRUCE B. FREEMAN

4 ATHERSTONE STREET · BOSTON, MASSACHUSETTS 02124
617 825-3768

CLIENT
The Flower Company
DESIGNER
Rochelle Seltzer
DESIGN FIRM
Rochelle Seltzer Design
MANUFACTURER
Smith Print
DESIGN AWARDS
American Corporate Identity 8

CLIENT
Eymer Design
DESIGNER
Douglas + Selene Eymer
DESIGN FIRM
Eymer Design
PRINTER
The Smith Print
ILLUSTRATOR
Douglas Eymer
TYPESETTER
Berkeley Typography
DESIGN AWARDS
Print
HOW
DESI
Corporate ID
MACTAC

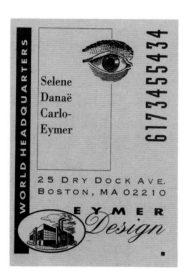

CLIENT
Leighton & Company
DESIGNER
Douglas Eymer
DESIGN FIRM
Eymer Design
PRINTER
The Smith Print
ILLUSTRATOR
Douglas Eymer
TYPESETTER
Berkeley Typography
PHOTOGRAPHER
Jeffrey Coolidge

CLIENT
Wendy Hebborn, Art Director
DESIGNER
Cary Michael Trout
DESIGN FIRM
Trout & Trout
TYPESETTER
Macintosh/Andresen Typographics
ILLUSTRATOR
Cary Trout

CLIENT
Rita's Catering
DESIGNER
Mark Oldach
DESIGN FIRM
Mark Oldach Design
MANUFACTURER
First Impression

CLIENT
John Joanette
DESIGNER
Mike Brotebeck
DESIGN FIRM
After Dinner Design
ILLUSTRATOR
Dover Archive
TYPESETTER
Great Faces, Inc.
DESIGN AWARDS
Gold—Addy Awards
Silver—TIA Awards

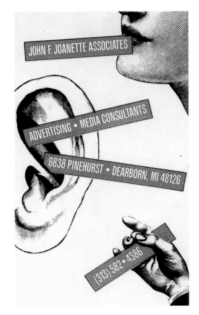

CLIENT
John Korinko Design
DESIGNER
John Korinko
DESIGN FIRM
John Korinko Design
ILLUSTRATOR
John Korinko
TYPESETTER
E. Fitz Art
DESIGN AWARDS
Art Directors Club of NJ 1991-Bronze Award
Beckett Paper Co. 1991 Award for Excellence

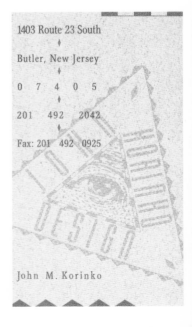

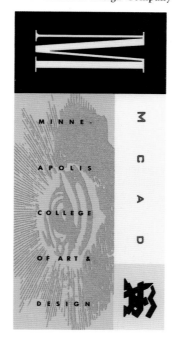

110 Wendy Lane
El Sobrante Ca
222-0873   94803

Ray Honda

CLIENT
Ray Honda
DESIGNER
Ray Honda
DESIGN FIRM
DMZ

CLIENT
Ray Honda
DESIGNER
Ray Honda
DESIGN FIRM
DMZ

CLIENT
Donny Honda, Thespian
DESIGNER
Ray Honda
DESIGN FIRM
DMZ

CLIENT
Garber Building Supplies Inc.
DESIGN FIRM
Reliable Design Studios, Inc.
TYPESETTER
Saxon Graphics
ILLUSTRATOR
Bill Kobasz

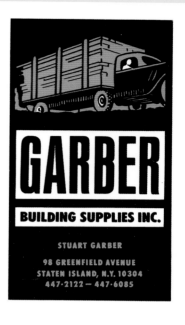

CLIENT
**Mike Salisbury
Communications, Inc.**
DESIGNER
**Cindy Luck
Mike Salisbury**
DESIGN FIRM
**Mike Salisbury
Communications, Inc.**
MANUFACTURER
King Printing
ILLUSTRATOR
Cindy Luck
TYPESETTER
CCI Typesetters

DESIGN AWARDS
GRAPHIS
PIE Books

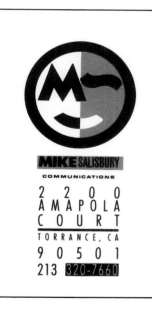

CLIENT
Post Industrial Press + Design
DESIGN FIRM
Art Chantry Design
TYPESETTER
Rockettype/Grant Alden

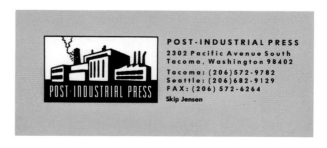

I'm John Kneapler, the one on the left.
Graphic/Corporate Design. 48 West 21
New York, New York 10010

BABY
FACE

MINNEAPOLIS

Cotton Play
for Infants

2518 Robbins
Minneapolis
55410

P. Jarvis
sident

SIGN & DISPLAY
CORP
TM
TRADE MARK

6th Ave. S., Seattle WA 98134
23.7676

SUSIE CUSHNER
.... Photography ....

G
T R
GREGORY T. RABIDEAU
ARCHITECT

Rosemary's Cakes

FLASH POINT

JOSEPH L. BUTT, Jr.
17 West 17th Street 1, NY, NY

6 York St. Jersey City 07302
077
48322
Jersey

DIRECTORY

Eleanor Bingham Mill

Lo
Kentu
502 893

354 Cong

Boston, MA 0

Fax:617 542-54

Falkirk Cultural Center

P.O. Box 15156 Street
915-15
Mission 94928

Frances Lee Jasper
Oriental Rugs

Photography

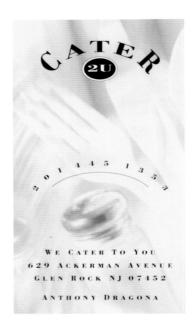

CLIENT
Susie Cushner Photography
DESIGNER
Melanie Lowe
DESIGN FIRM
Clifford Selbert Design
PRINTER
Alpha Press
TYPESETTER
Clifford Selbert Design
PHOTOGRAPHER
Susie Cushner

CLIENT
Hat Life Directory
DESIGNER
Alex Bonziglia
DESIGN FIRM
David Morris Design Associates
MANUFACTURER
Dohrman Printing
TYPESETTER
Alex Bonziglia
PHOTOGRAPHER
Scott Wippermann

CLIENT
Cater 2U
DESIGNER
Kurt Jennings
DESIGN FIRM
Kurt Jennings
PRINTER
Impressions, Inc.
TYPESETTER
Kurt Jennings- Aldus Freehand on
Macintosh
PHOTOGRAPHER
Tracy Alen Aiken
DESIGN AWARDS
Arjomari Paper Competition—
Second Place for use of "trophy"
coated paper

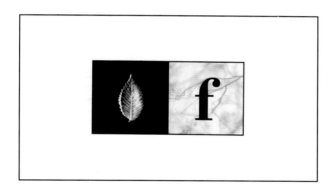

ABBIE SEWALL

Photography

11 North Elm Street
Yarmouth, Maine 04096   207 846 5835

CLIENT
Abbie Sewall Photography
DESIGN FIRM
Designsense
PHOTOGRAPHER
© 1991 Abbie Sewall

Falkirk Cultural Center

P.O. Box 151560
1408 Mission at E Street
San Rafael, Ca 94915-1560
Tel: 415 485 3328
Fax: 415 485 3112

CLIENT
Falkirk Cultural Center
DESIGNER
Tom Bonauro
DESIGN FIRM
Tom Bonauro Design
MANUFACTURER
Logos Graphics
PHOTOGRAPHER
Jeffery Newbury

CLIENT
Art Kane Studio, Inc.
DESIGNER
Mike Quon
Eileen Kinneary
DESIGN FIRM
Mike Quon Design Office
DESIGN AWARDS
Creativity

ART KANE STUDIO, INC.

568 BROADWAY · NY, NY 10012 · TEL. 212 925 7334
FAX 212 966 7987

CLIENT
Gregory T. Rabideau
DESIGNER
Christopher M. Reck
DESIGN FIRM
Direct Design
MANUFACTURER
PIP Printing
TYPESETTER
Christopher M. Reck
ILLUSTRATOR
Christopher M. Reck
DESIGN AWARDS
Mohawk Paper Mills—Certificate
of Merit

CLIENT
Willingtown Construction
Pete Sanger
DESIGNER
Tony Ross
DESIGN FIRM
Ross Design Inc.
PHOTOGRAPHER
Bob Prengle
ILLUSTRATOR
Tony Ross
TYPESETTER
Macintosh
DESIGN AWARDS
Print Magazine
Ad Club of Delaware

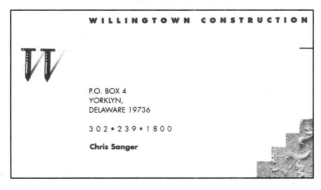

WILLINGTOWN CONSTRUCTION

P.O. BOX 4
YORKLYN,
DELAWARE 19736

302 · 239 · 1800

Chris Sanger

CLIENT
The Salvage Crew
DESIGNER
Rick Tharp
DESIGN FIRM
THARP DID IT
PRINTER
West Valley Graphics
PHOTOGRAPHER
Kelly O' Connor
TYPESETTER
FotoComp

CLIENT
Samenwerkende Ontwerpers
DESIGNER
Simon Davies
DESIGN FIRM
Samenwerkende Ontwerpers
MANUFACTURER
Drukkerij Mart. Spruijt
PHOTOGRAPHER
Simon Davies
ILLUSTRATOR
Simon Davies
TYPESETTER
Drukkerij Mart. Spruijt

CLIENT
Kent Marshall Photography
DESIGNER
Cameron Woo
DESIGN FIRM
Cameron Woo Design
PHOTOGRAPHER
Kent Marshall

KENT MARSHALL
PHOTOGRAPHY

ADVERTISING
EDITORIAL
PORTRAITURE

SAN FRANCISCO
CALIFORNIA
☎ OFFICE 415.738.9306
STUDIO 415.641.0932
FAX 415.738.0354

CLIENT
Rosemary's Cakes
DESIGNER
Wallace Littman
DESIGN FIRM
W. Littman Design
PHOTOGRAPHER
Barry Seidman

CLIENT
Flash Point
DESIGNER
Linda Pierro
DESIGN FIRM
D-Zine, Inc.
TYPESETTER
Carl Waltzer Typography
PHOTOGRAPHER
Jim Zuckerman
DESIGN AWARDS
DESI Award

FLASH▼POINT

JOSEPH L. BUTT, Jr.

17 West 17th Street ▼ NY, NY 10011 ▼ TEL 212 645 9113 ▼ FAX 212 645 0499

CLIENT
Eleanor Bingham Miller
DESIGNER
Walter McCord
DESIGN FIRM
Walter McCord Graphic Design
MANUFACTURER
Hamilton Printing
PHOTOGRAPHER
Eadweard Muybridge
TYPESETTER
Harlan Typographic
DESIGN AWARDS
Print, Letterheads 6

Eleanor Bingham Miller   Producer

6408 Longview Lane
Louisville,
Kentucky 40222
502 893 2262

ROSEMARY'S CAKES

Rosemary Littman

299 Rutland Ave.
Teaneck, New Jersey 07666
201-833-2417

CLIENT
Ray Honda
DESIGNER
Ray Honda
DESIGN FIRM
DMZ

CLIENT
Baby Face Children's Playwear
DESIGNER
J. Graham Hanson
MANUFACTURER
Quick Print Minneapolis
TYPESETTER
J. Graham Hanson
PHOTOGRAPHER
Jeremy Clifford

CLIENT
Machine Head
DESIGNER
Lorna Stovall
DESIGN FIRM
Lorna Stovall
TYPESETTER
Type, Inc.

CLIENT
Trade-Mark Sign & Display Corp.
DESIGNER
Rick Eiber
DESIGN FIRM
Rick Eiber Design (RED)
MANUFACTURER
Artcraft Printing
ILLUSTRATOR
Norman Hathaway
TYPESETTER
The Type Gallery

CLIENT
Carol DeLong
DESIGNER
Bart Crosby
DESIGN FIRM
Crosby Associates Inc.
PHOTOGRAPHER
Bart Crosby
TYPESETTER
Typographic Resource, Ltd.

The Pleasure is All Mime, **Carol DeLong**, Mime

1358 W. Greenleaf, Chicago 60626 312.274.3534

CLIENT
Frances Lee Jasper Oriental Rugs
DESIGNER
Walter McCord
DESIGN FIRM
Walter McCord Graphic Design
MANUFACTURER
Hamilton Printing
TYPESETTER
Harlan Typographic
PHOTOGRAPHER
Marian Klein Koehler
DESIGN AWARDS
Print

Frances Lee Jasper
Oriental Rugs

Quad 7
1330 Bardstown Road
Louisville
Kentucky 40204
502 459-1044

I'm John Kneapler, the one on the left.
Graphic/Corporate Design. 48 West 21st 12th fl.
New York, New York 10010 (212) 463-9774

CLIENT
John Kneapler
DESIGNER
John Kneapler
DESIGN FIRM
John Kneapler Design
PHOTOGRAPHER
Charles Kneapler
(Dad) circa 1958

Typography & Logos

CHRIS WOLLERMAN

4740 Grand

Kansas City, Missouri

64112

(816) 561-8000

CLIENT
PB & J Restaurants: Grand St. Cafe
DESIGNER
Patrice Eilts
DESIGN FIRM
Eilts, Anderson & Tracy Design
MANUFACTURER
Cicero Graphic Resources and
BearPrint
TYPESETTER
Rich Kobs on Macintosh
ILLUSTRATOR
Patrice Eilts
Rich Kobs
DESIGN AWARDS
Gold—Kansas City Art Directors
*International Menu Design
Annual*

SUNDOG PRODUCTIONS

THOMAS POLLARD
9 WALNUT AVENUE   ANDOVER, MA 01810   (508) 474 0905

CLIENT
Sundog Productions
DESIGNER
Jeff Pollard
DESIGN FIRM
Pollard Design
PRINTER
The Pond-Ekberg Company
DESIGN AWARDS
*1991 Communication Arts Design
Annual*

CLIENT
Brainstorm Unlimited
DESIGNER
Richard Bruning
Dean Motter
DESIGN FIRM
Brainstorm Unlimited
PRINTER
Colonial Printing

CLIENT
Newbury Filmworks, Inc.
DESIGNER
Marc English
DESIGN FIRM
Marc English Design
MANUFACTURER
Condor Litho

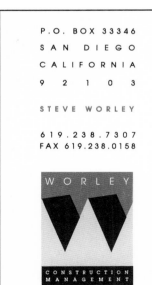

CLIENT
Worley Construction Management
DESIGNER
Tyler Blik
Anita Frederick
Ken Soto
DESIGN FIRM
Tyler Blik Design Associates
MANUFACTURER
DeFrance Printing
TYPESETTER
Macintosh
DESIGN AWARDS
Communication Arts Group,
San Diego
Print's Regional Design Annual

PAUL STUART RANKIN, *Inc.*

50 BANK STREET NEW YORK, NEW YORK 10014

2 1 2 727·3869

CLIENT
Paul Stuart Rankin, Inc.
Interior Design
DESIGNER
Richard Manville
DESIGN FIRM
Manville Bakacs Santana
MANUFACTURER
Charlton & Charlton Lithographers

white+associates

marketing design
and advertising
137
north virgil avenue
suite 204
los angeles
california
90004-4848

213 380-6319
213 380-3427 fax

CLIENT
White + Associates-Marketing
Design and Advertising
DESIGNER
Kristen Jester
DESIGN FIRM
White + Associates

CLIENT
Phillip Johnson Assoc., Inc.
DESIGNER
Douglas Eymer
DESIGN FIRM
Eymer Design
PRINTER
Maran Printing
ILLUSTRATOR
Douglas Eymer
TYPESETTER
Berkeley Typographers
DESIGN AWARDS
Creative Club of Boston

Linda Chryle writes.

Linda Chryle lives.
843 West Van Buren
No. 211
Chicago, Illinois
60607

Linda Chryle talks.
312.733.1124

And she faxes, too.
312.733.1125

CLIENT
Linda Chryle Writes
DESIGNER
Mark Oldach
DESIGN FIRM
Mark Oldach Design
TYPESETTER
Mastertype

THE BOW GROUP

12 ARROW STREET
CAMBRIDGE, MA 02138

TEL: 617 661 7513
FAX: 617 661 1530

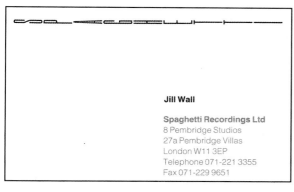

Jill Wall

Spaghetti Recordings Ltd
8 Pembridge Studios
27a Pembridge Villas
London W11 3EP
Telephone 071-221 3355
Fax 071-229 9651

CLIENT
Spaghetti Recordings Ltd.
DESIGNER
David Hillman
DESIGN FIRM
Pentagram Design Ltd.
MANUFACTURER
Kidford Printers

CLIENT
The Leonard Designship
DESIGNER
Katherine Nemec
MANUFACTURER
CEI Printing

the leonard designship

861 North

• 22nd St. Philadelphia, PA 19130 • 215.236.4770

KURT JENNINGS DESIGN

53 BONN PLACE

WEEHAWKEN, NEW JERSEY

07087

TELEPHONE 201.865.8641

CLIENT
Kurt Jennings Design
DESIGNER
Kurt Jennings
DESIGN FIRM
Kurt Jennings
MANUFACTURER
Classic Reprographics, Inc.
TYPESETTER
Macintosh—Quark Xpress

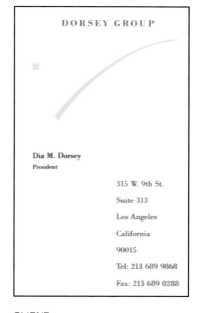

DORSEY GROUP

Dia M. Dorsey
President

315 W. 9th St.

Suite 313

Los Angeles

California

90015

Tel: 213 689 9868

Fax: 213 689 0288

CLIENT
Dorsey Group
DESIGNER
John Coy
Laurie Handler
DESIGN FIRM
COY, Los Angeles
MANUFACTURER
The Paper Blizzard
TYPESETTER
Aldus Type Studio, Ltd.

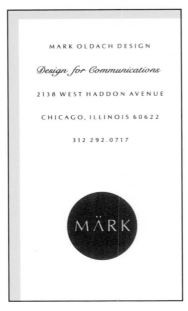

MARK OLDACH DESIGN

Design for Communications

2138 WEST HADDON AVENUE

CHICAGO, ILLINOIS 60622

312 292.0717

MÄRK

CLIENT
Mark Oldach Design
DESIGNER
Mark Oldach
DESIGN FIRM
Mark Oldach Design
MANUFACTURER
First Impression
TYPESETTER
The Typecasters

CLIENT
Michael Weaver Illustration
DESIGNER
Patrice Eilts
DESIGN FIRM
Eilts, Anderson & Tracy Design
MANUFACTURER
Constable Hodgins Printers
TYPESETTER
Hand type: Patrice Eilts
Lopez Graphics
ILLUSTRATOR
Patrice Eilts
DESIGN AWARDS
Typography 12
A Decade of Type
PIE *International Business*
Stationery
PIE *International Logos*
Gold—Kansas City Art Directors

CLIENT
COY, Los Angeles
DESIGNER
John Coy
DESIGN FIRM
COY, Los Angeles
MANUFACTURER
S & P Printing
TYPESETTER
Continental Typographics

CLIENT
Ristorante Ecco
DESIGNER
Jennifer Morla
Craig Bailey
DESIGN FIRM
Morla Design, Inc.
MANUFACTURER
Wright Printing
ILLUSTRATOR
Jennifer Morla
TYPESETTER
Jennifer Morla (hand-lettering)

Cobalt
Real Estate
Investment
Corporation

101 South Park

San Francisco

CA 94107

415.495.3291

9 1 5
West Huron Street
Chicago, Illinois
6 0 6 2 2

T E L   312 421.0004
F A X   312 421.1294

CLIENT
Cobalt
DESIGNER
Mark Oldach
DESIGN FIRM
Mark Oldach Design

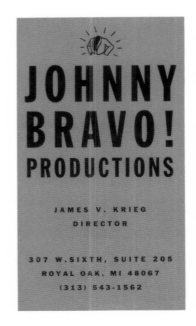

JAMES V. KRIEG
DIRECTOR

307 W.SIXTH, SUITE 205
ROYAL OAK, MI 48067
(313) 543-1562

CLIENT
Johnny Bravo! Productions
DESIGNER
Fritz Klaetke
DESIGN FIRM
Visual Dialogue
MANUFACTURER
The Print House
TYPESETTER
Graphics Express
ILLUSTRATOR
Polly Becker

CLIENT
QC Graphics
DESIGNER
Rick Vaughn
DESIGN FIRM
Vaughn/Wedeen Creative
PRINTER
Albuquerque Printing
ILLUSTRATOR
Rick Vaughn
DESIGN AWARDS
PIE Books—*Business Card Design*

CLIENT
Bumble + Bumble
DESIGNER
Mike Quon
Eileen Kinneary
DESIGN FIRM
Mike Quon Design Office
DESIGN AWARDS
DESI/Creativity

CLIENT
Lilly's
DESIGNER
Walter McCord
DESIGN FIRM
Walter McCord Graphic Design
MANUFACTURER
Cardinal Lithographing
ILLUSTRATOR
Walter McCord
TYPESETTER
Derby City Litho
DESIGN AWARDS
Menu Design

RAMSTONE

Barie McCurry
Vice President

2504 Camino Entrada
Santa Fe, NM 87505
505·473·9419
800·635·7551
FAX·505·473·5519

A Division of Advanced Design Technologies

CLIENT
Ramstone
DESIGNER
Steve Wedeen
Dan Flynn
DESIGN FIRM
Vaughn/Wedeen Creative
PRINTER
Albuquerque Printing
ILLUSTRATOR
Rick Vaughn
DESIGN AWARDS
Local Addy Award

PLANET U&A

PLANNING
NETWORKING
URBANISM
ARCHITECTURE

常務取締役
石 井 寛 美
〒107 東京都港区北青山3-5-8 水田ビル7F
Tel. 03-3796-7791
Fax. 03-3796-7793

CLIENT
Planet U & A
DESIGNER
U.G. Sato
DESIGN FIRM
Design Farm Inc.
MANUFACTURER
Yoshioka Printing Co., Ltd.
ILLUSTRATOR
U.G. Sato

CLIENT
mla haus
DESIGNER
Jann Church
DESIGN FIRM
Jann Church Partners Advertising &
Graphic Design

mla·haus

This house cares for other houses. With an understanding of construction methods, materials and environments, mla·haus provides varied remodeling services for homes, offices, restaurants, and stores. Construction services range from initial design and consultation through permits and approvals. Materials are purposefully selected to enrich the intent of the design. The art of remodeling when applied by the mla·haus system will result in efficient and cost-effective construction additions. The tools of our craft are housed at 17848 Sky Park Boulevard, Irvine, CA 92714 (714) 556-6610.

Mark Cernich

MANTAGARIS

GALLERIES

77 GEARY STREET

SAN FRANCISCO

CALIFORNIA 94108

415.398.5475

LINDA JACOBS MANTOS

CLIENT
Mantagaris Galleries
DESIGNER
Cheryl Harrison
DESIGN FIRM
Harrison Design Group
MANUFACTURER
Foreman Liebrock
TYPESETTER
Linotronic Output/Pinnacle Type
ILLUSTRATOR
Robert Mesarchik

OMEGA
ENTERPRISES
INC.

KAREN R. BOND
SECRETARY/TREASURER

3616 MATEO PRADO NW
ALBUQUERQUE, NM 87107
505/345-9474

CLIENT
Omega Enterprises Inc.
DESIGNER
Dan Flynn
DESIGN FIRM
Flynn Graphic Design
PRINTER
Academy Printers
TYPESETTER
Typesavers
DESIGN AWARDS
Neenah Paper
Honor Award Letterhead Design

LINDA GRAF
Print Representative

1417 Bridgeway #1
P.O. Box 1735
Sausalito
California 94966

Telephone:
415.331.1657
Facsimile:
415.332.3990

CLIENT
Linda Graf
DESIGNER
Thomas McNulty
Brian Jacobson
DESIGN FIRM
Profile Design
TYPESETTER
Spartan Type
DESIGN AWARDS
Print Magazine

Design

Lam & Company

130 West 25 Street

New York NY 10001

212.675.6155

Fax.989.2845

CLIENT
Lam & Company
DESIGNER
Henry Lam
DESIGN FIRM
Lam & Company

CLIENT
Golf Enterprises, Inc.
ART DIRECTOR
John White
DESIGNER
John White
Aram Youssefian
DESIGN FIRM
White Design
PRINTER
A.R.T. Printing & Graphics
TYPESETTER
Composition Type

GOLF ENTERPRISES, INC.

1448 15th Street, Suite 200
Santa Monica, California 90404
213/576-6020
Fax 213/576-6030

Richard Eskite

Richard Eskite Photography
2343 3rd Street, Suite 295 ★ Telephone 415.626.9606
San Francisco, Ca. 94107

CLIENT
Richard Eskite Photography
DESIGNER
Thomas McNulty
Kenichi Nishiwaki
DESIGN FIRM
Profile Design
TYPESETTER
Spartan Type

Jeff Johnson

63-B Maverick Square #11
East Boston, Massachusetts 02128
(617) 567-5293

CLIENT
Jeff Johnson
DESIGNER
Jeff Johnson
DESIGN FIRM
Jeff Johnson
MANUFACTURER
American Speedy Printing

AMERICAN
TAILORING

Patty Gum

11322 Camarillo St. No. 304
North Hollywood, CA 91602

818 980 5114
FAX 818 505 1199

CLIENT
American Tailoring
ART DIRECTOR
Larry Vigon
DESIGNERS
Larry Vigon
Brian Jackson
DESIGN FIRM
Larry Vigon Studio
ILLUSTRATOR
Larry Vigon

CLIENT
Ben Liberty
DESIGNER
Gail Rigelhaupt
DESIGN FIRM
Rigelhaupt Design

CLIENT
Kronen Audio
DESIGNER
Steve Wedeen
DESIGN FIRM
Vaughn/Wedeen Creative
PRINTER
Academy Printing
DESIGN AWARDS
Print's Regional Design Annual
GRAPHIS Letterhead 1

CLIENT
Ilene Shaw
The Shaw Corp.
DESIGNER
Gail Rigelhaupt
DESIGN FIRM
Rigelhaupt Design

CLIENT
Pisarkiewicz & Co., Inc.
DESIGNER
Mary F. Pisarkiewicz
DESIGN FIRM
Pisarkiewicz & Co., Inc.
TYPESETTER
M & D
DESIGN AWARDS
Creativity 1991

abcdefghijklmnopisarkiewicz

A comprehensive communication design agency.

Mary F. Pisarkiewicz
President

• Pisarkiewicz & Co., Inc.
• 34 West 22nd Street
• New York, N.Y. 10010
• Phone 212·645·6265
• Fax 212·645·6369

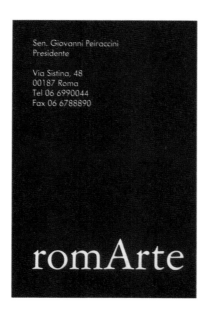

Sen. Giovanni Peiraccini
Presidente

Via Sistina, 48
00187 Roma
Tel 06 6990044
Fax 06 6788890

romArte

CLIENT
romArte
DESIGNER
John McConnell
DESIGN FIRM
Pentagram Design Ltd.
MANUFACTURER
Gavin Martin Ltd.

400 Market Street
Suite 1225
Philadelphia, PA 19106
(215) 925-4462

American Music Theater
FESTIVAL

CLIENT
American Music Theater Festival
DESIGNER
Gail Rigelhaupt
Tom Dolle
DESIGN FIRM
Design Squad

CLIENT
Houk Friedman Gallery
DESIGNER
Eric Baker
DESIGN FIRM
Eric Baker Design Associates, Inc.

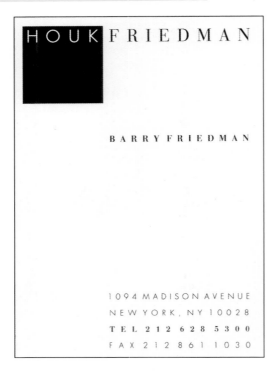

CLIENT
Morla Design
DESIGNER
Jennifer Morla
DESIGN FIRM
Morla Design
MANUFACTURER
Williams Lithograph Co.
Zablocki-Olympic Co.
TYPESETTER
Spartan Typographers, Inc.
DESIGN AWARDS
GRAPHIS **Letterhead Design '91**

CLIENT
Allyson Anthony
DESIGNER
Jennifer Morla
Jeanette Aramburu
DESIGN FIRM
Morla Design
MANUFACTURER
Golden Dragon Printing
TYPESETTER
Spartan Typographers, Inc.

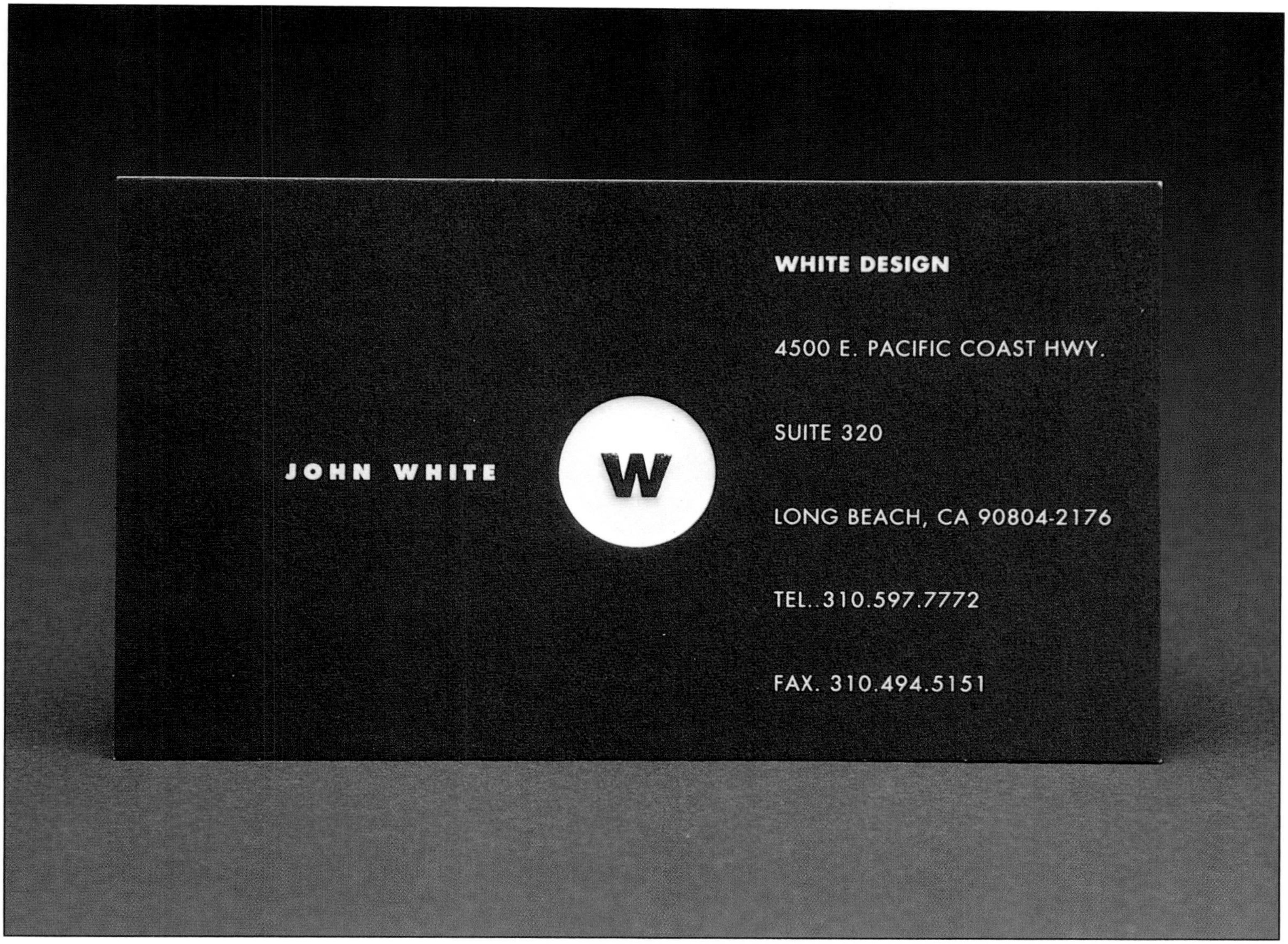

WHITE DESIGN

4500 E. PACIFIC COAST HWY.

SUITE 320

LONG BEACH, CA 90804-2176

TEL..310.597.7772

FAX. 310.494.5151

JOHN WHITE

CLIENT
White Design
ART DIRECTOR
John White
DESIGNER
John White
Aram Youssefian
DESIGN FIRM
White Design
PRINTER
A.R.T. Printing & Graphics
TYPESETTER
Composition Type

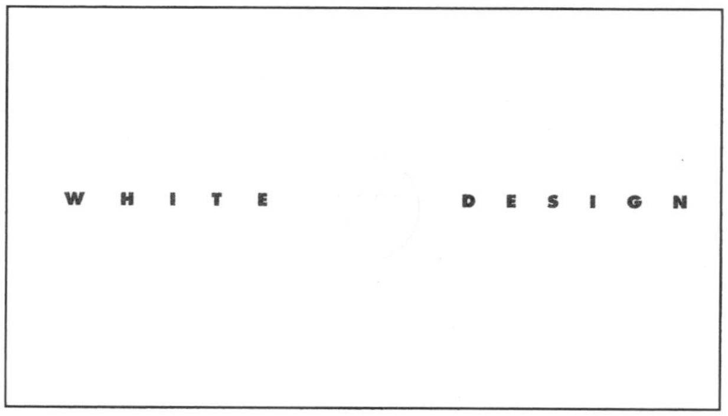

WHITE DESIGN

CLIENT
Sourelis + Associates
DESIGNER
Mark Oldach
DESIGN FIRM
Mark Oldach Design
MANUFACTURER
Davidson Group

CLIENT
New York Pride
DESIGNER
Kurt Jennings
DESIGN FIRM
Bright & Associates, Inc.
MANUFACTURER
Tanagraphics, Inc.
HAND LETTERING
Taro Yamashita

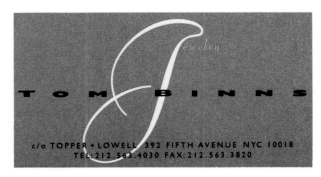

CLIENT
Tom Binns Jewelry
DESIGNER
Gail Rigelhaupt
Tom Binns
DESIGN FIRM
Rigelhaupt Design

CLIENT
Parker & James Communications
DESIGNER
Robert C. Downing
DESIGN FIRM
Downing & Filzow/Graphic Design
TYPESETTER
Downing & Filzow/Graphic Design

CLIENT
National Air + Space Museum,
Smithsonian Institution
DESIGNER
Gail Rigelhaupt
DESIGN FIRM
Rigelhaupt Design

CLIENT
Thomas J. McVety
DESIGNER
Thomas J. McVety
TYPESETTER
Thomas J. McVety

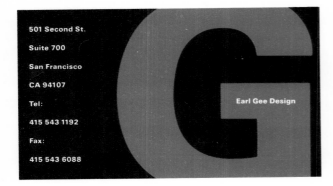

501 Second St.

Suite 700

San Francisco

CA 94107

Tel:

415 543 1192

Fax:

415 543 6088

Earl Gee Design

CLIENT
Earl Gee Design
DESIGNER
Earl Gee
DESIGN FIRM
Earl Gee Design
ILLUSTRATOR
Earl Gee
TYPESETTER
Z Typography

CLIENT
Evie Avinante & Associates
DESIGNER
Tyler Blik
Ken Soto
DESIGN FIRM
Tyler Blik Design Associates
MANUFACTURER
DeFrance Printing
TYPESETTER
Macintosh

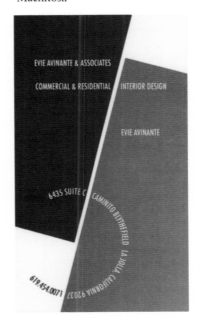

FANI CHUNG DESIGN

501 SECOND STREET, SUITE 700

SAN FRANCISCO, CA 94107

TEL : 415 · 512 · 7080

FAX : 415 · 543 · 6088

CLIENT
Fani Chung Design
DESIGNER
Fani Chung
DESIGN FIRM
Fani Chung Design
TYPESETTER
Z Typography

CLIENT
Lisa Levin Design
DESIGNER
Lisa Levin
DESIGN FIRM
Lisa Levin Design
MANUFACTURER
Julie Holcomb Printing
TYPESETTER
Macintosh
DESIGN AWARDS
The San Francisco Show 4

CLIENT
Center For The Arts, Yerba
Buena Gardens
DESIGNER
Lucille Tenazas
DESIGN FIRM
Tenazas Design
MANUFACTURER
Expressions Lithography
TYPESETTER
Eurotype

CLIENT
William Taufic Photography Inc.
DESIGNER
Brian E. Baufin
Wayne C. Roth
DESIGN FIRM
Roth + Associates
TYPESETTER
Brian E. Boutin (Desktop)

CLIENT
Little City Restaurant & Antipasti
Bar
DESIGNER
Bruce Yelaska
DESIGN FIRM
Bruce Yelaska Design
MANUFACTURER
S.F. Lithographics
TYPESETTER
CityType
DESIGN AWARDS
Print's Regional Design Annual
American Corp. Identity
Menu Design 3
Print's Best Letterheads &
Business Cards
Business Card Graphics (PIE
Books)
Trademarks of the 1980's
The Washington Trademark Project

CLIENT
Adriane Stark
DESIGNER
Adriane Stark
DESIGN FIRM
Stark Design Associates
DESIGN AWARDS
The Golden Quill Awards—Silver

CLIENT
Sean Adams
DESIGNER
Sean Adams
DESIGN FIRM
Sean Adams
MANUFACTURER
Monarch Litho

MARK ZINGARELLI

8217 CEDARHOME DRIVE, STANWOOD, WASHINGTON 98292
8217 CEDARHOME DRIVE, STANWOOD, WASHINGTON
8217 CEDARHOME DRIVE, STA...

TEL (206) 629-3696
FAX (206) 629-4682
TEL (206) 629-3696

CLIENT
Mark Zingarelli Illustration
DESIGN FIRM
Art Chantry Design
TYPESETTER
Rockettype/Grant Alden

CLIENT
David Zander Furniture
DESIGNER
Vincent Romeo
DESIGN FIRM
Romeo Empire Design
PRINTER
Tanner Durso, Inc.
ILLUSTRATOR
Vincent Romeo

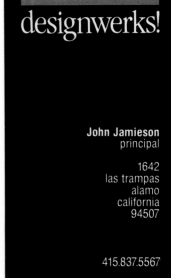

designwerks!

John Jamieson
principal

1642
las trampas
alamo
california
94507

415.837.5567

CLIENT
Designwerks!
DESIGNER
John Jamieson
DESIGN FIRM
Designwerks!
PRINTER
Graphic Impressions
TYPESETTER
Brooks Typography

CLIENT
Antero Ferreira Design
DESIGNER
Antero Ferreira
DESIGN FIRM
Antero Ferreira
MANUFACTURER
Marca Artes Gráficas

CLIENT
Barbara Kurgan
DESIGNER
Bill Kobasz
DESIGN FIRM
Reliable Design Studios, Inc.
TYPESETTER
Saxon Graphics

CLIENT
Anton Grassl Photographie
DESIGNER
Robin Perkins
DESIGN FIRM
Clifford Selbert Design
PRINTER
Star Litho
TYPESETTER
Clifford Selbert Design

CLIENT
Drukkerij Mart. Spruijt
DESIGNER
Marianne Vos
DESIGN FIRM
Samenwerkende Ontwerpers
MANUFACTURER
Drukkerij Mart. Spruijt
TYPESETTER
Drukkerij Mart. Spruijt
DESIGN AWARDS
D & AD, 1989

Rebetez
Bäumleingasse 10   CH 4051 Basel

Telephon 061-23 31 80
Telex 62 611 reb ch

Christine Rebetez
Geschäftsführerin

CLIENT
Rebetez, Fine Papers and
Art Supplies
DESIGNER
Douglas Davie
DESIGN FIRM
Davie and Lindholm Design
Partnership
MANUFACTURER
AGS
TYPESETTER
Davie/Weingart
ILLUSTRATOR
Davie/Hofmann

Karen Guancione
Art & Design
262 De Witt Ave.
Belleville, NJ 07109
201 • 759 • 4703

CLIENT
Karen Guancione
DESIGNER
Karen Guancione
DESIGN FIRM
Karen Guancione Art & Design

CLIENT
Richard Rogers Partnership
DESIGNER
Alan Fletcher
DESIGN FIRM
Pentagram Design Ltd.
MANUFACTURER
Jaguar Press Ltd.

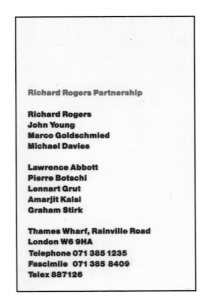

Richard Rogers Partnership

Richard Rogers
John Young
Marco Goldschmied
Michael Davies

Lawrence Abbott
Pierre Botschi
Lennart Grut
Amarjit Kaisi
Graham Stirk

Thames Wharf, Rainville Road
London W6 9HA
Telephone 071 385 1235
Fascimile 071 385 8409
Telex 887126

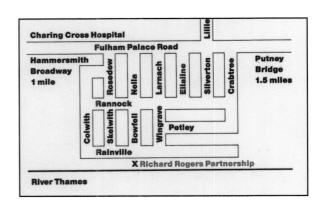

KATHY WARINNER

AUFULDISH & WARINNER

graphic designers

104 william ave larkspur ca 94939

415 927 8128

CLIENT
Aufuldish & Warinner
DESIGNER
Kathy Warinner
Bob Aufuldish
DESIGN FIRM
Aufuldish & Warinner
PRINTER
Logos Graphics
TYPESETTER
A & W

BOB AUFULDISH

AUFULDISH & WARINNER

graphic designers

104 william ave larkspur ca 94939

415 927 8128

CLIENT
**Barnes Brandt and Josephson
Partners, Inc.**
DESIGNER
Liisa Lindholm
Douglas Davie
DESIGN FIRM
**Davie and Lindholm Design
Partnership**
ILLUSTRATOR
Liisa Lindholm
Douglas Davie

The
COMMUNIQUÉ GROUP, Inc.

Advertising, Marketing, Promotions

42 Glen Avenue
Newton Centre, MA 02159
617·527·2230

Laurie Lewis Carlson
Production Coordinator

CLIENT
The Communiqué Group
DESIGNER
Karen Watkins
DESIGN FIRM
Ruby Shoes Studio
DESIGN AWARDS
Cranes Certificate of Excellence

Roslyn Brandt

**Barnes Brandt and Josephson
Partners, Inc.**

Investment Banking for the
Design and Furnishings Community

885 Third Avenue
New York, New York 10022-4802

Facsimile: 212 230-3256
Telephone: 212 230-3235

The Type Gallery, Inc.

1121 Westlake Avenue North
Seattle, Washington 98109
Phone (206) 285-6333

Betty Handly
President

CLIENT
The Type Gallery, Inc.
DESIGNER
Rick Eiber
DESIGN FIRM
Rick Eiber Design (RED)
MANUFACTURER
Artcraft Printing
TYPESETTER
The Type Gallery, Inc.

Two North Park Suite 600
8080 Park Lane
Dallas, Texas 75231
214.340.3400

J. Michael Roach

CLIENT
Lincx Incorporated
DESIGNER
Marcos Chavez
DESIGN FIRM
Michael Stanard, Incorporated

CLIENT
Milton Glaser, Inc.
DESIGNER
Milton Glaser
DESIGN FIRM
Milton Glaser, Inc.
TYPESETTER
Cardinal

MILTON GLASER, INCORPORATED   TEL: (212) 889-3161

207

E. 32 ST., NEW YORK 10016

ARTICLE 19
INTERNATIONAL CENTRE AGAINST CENSORSHIP

Susan Hay
Bulletin Editor and
Membership
Co-ordinator

90 Borough High St.
London SE1 1LL
United Kingdom
Telephone:
071-403 4822
Facsimile:
071-403 1943

CLIENT
International Centre Against
Censorship
DESIGNER
David Hillman
DESIGN FIRM
Pentagram Design Ltd.
MANUFACTURER
Calverts Press

Kevin Harvey
President & CEO

APPROACH

Approach Software
311 Penobscot Drive
Redwood City, CA 94063
Tel: 415.306.7890
Fax: 415.368.5182

CLIENT
Approach Software
DESIGNER
Anthony Luk
Thomas McNulty
DESIGN FIRM
Profile Design
MANUFACTURER
Software Company
TYPESETTER
Spartan Type
DESIGN AWARDS
HOW Magazine

S T A C I

W H I T E

818·545·8554

STACIWHITEINTERIORDESI
GNANDCONSULTING122SOUT
HCEDARSTREETNUMBERTEN,G
LENDALE,CALIFORNIA91205

CLIENT
Staci White Interior Design
DESIGNER
Ken White
DESIGN FIRM
White + Associates
ILLUSTRATOR
Jessie McAnulty

CLIENT
DMZ
DESIGNER
Ray Honda
DESIGN FIRM
DMZ

RAY HONDA

477 PACIFIC AVENUE

SAN FRANCISCO

9   4   1   3   3

T : 415 397 0231

F : 415 397 0129

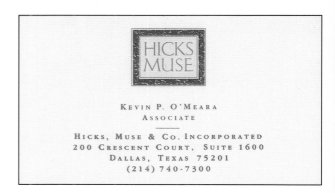

HICKS
MUSE

KEVIN P. O'MEARA
ASSOCIATE

HICKS, MUSE & CO. INCORPORATED
200 CRESCENT COURT, SUITE 1600
DALLAS, TEXAS 75201
(214) 740-7300

CLIENT
Hicks Muse & Co. Incorporated
DESIGNER
Bob Dennard
Chuck Johnson
DESIGN FIRM
Dennard Creative Inc.
MANUFACTURER
Fine Arts Engraving &
Monarch Press
TYPESETTER
Image Type
DESIGN AWARDS
Dallas Ad League—Tops Award

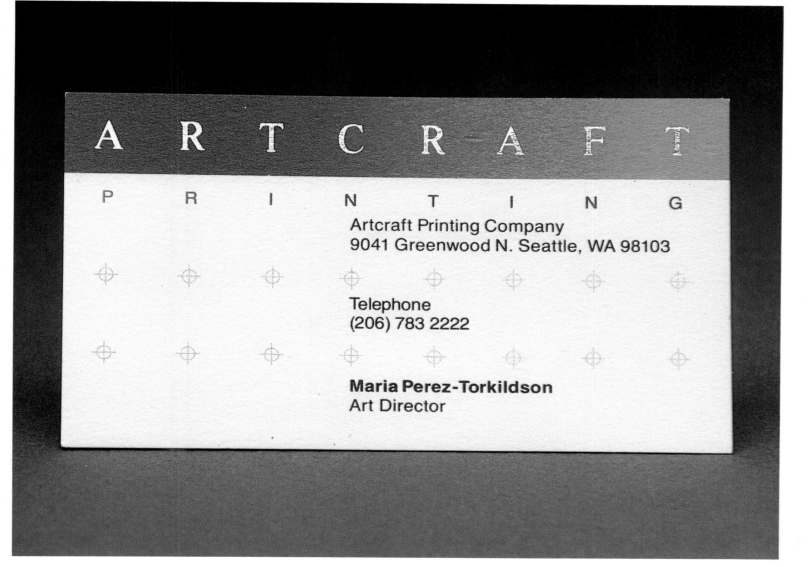

ARTCRAFT
PRINTING

Artcraft Printing Company
9041 Greenwood N. Seattle, WA 98103

Telephone
(206) 783 2222

Maria Perez-Torkildson
Art Director

CLIENT
Artcraft Printing Co.
DESIGNER
Rick Eiber
DESIGN FIRM
Rick Eiber Design (RED)
MANUFACTURER
Artcraft Printing Co.
TYPESETTER
The Type Gallery

CLIENT
Michael Shepley
Public Relations
DESIGNER
J. Drew Hodges
DESIGN FIRM
Spot Design
MANUFACTURER
Canfield Press

CLIENT
C.S. Anderson Design Company
DESIGNER
Charles S. Anderson
Daniel Olson
DESIGN FIRM
C.S. Anderson Design Company

CLIENT
Joannie B. Ames
DESIGNER
Joannie B. Ames
DESIGN FIRM
Full Circle Graphics

CLIENT
Richard Hand
Tree Service
DESIGNER
Catherine A. Vogel
DESIGN FIRM
Catherine Vogel Design

CLIENT
Jack Rizzo Computer Aided Design
DESIGNER
Jack C. Rizzo
DESIGN FIRM
Jack Rizzo Computer Aided Design

CLIENT
Axiom, Inc.
DESIGNER
Walter McCord
DESIGN FIRM
Walter McCord Graphic Design
MANUFACTURER
Lipps National Printers
ILLUSTRATOR
Walter McCord
TYPESETTER
Harlan Typographic
DESIGN AWARDS
Type Directors Club, 1991

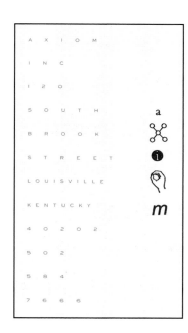

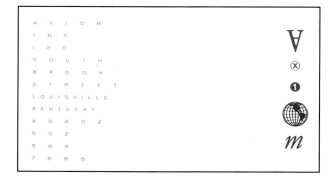

CRAIG CUTLER STUDIO, INC.

628-30 BROADWAY

NEW YORK, NY 10012

PHONE 212-473-2892

FAX 212-473-8306

CRAIG CUTLER

CLIENT
Craig Cutler Studio, Inc.
DESIGNER
Greg Simpson
DESIGN FIRM
The Pushpin Group, Inc.
TYPESETTER
Pulsar

Bb

Bridget Barry
COPYWRITER
(817) 292-5764

5025 Overton Ridge Cir., #1728
Fort Worth, TX 76132

CLIENT
Bridget Barry, copywriter
DESIGNER
Candice Swanson
DESIGN FIRM
Candice Swanson On Call
TYPESETTER
Letraset and Typeworks of Dallas
DESIGN AWARDS
Print's Regional Design Annual—
Certificate of Design Excellence

**Blah
Blah
Blah**

jeff walker • ad guy
414•962•3664

CLIENT
Jeff Walker
DESIGNER
Todd Brei
DESIGN FIRM
Quinn Brei
PRINTER
Clark Graphics
TYPESETTER
Macintosh Classic & Apple
Stylewriter

2806 W. 49TH TERR

SHAWNEE MISSION

KANSAS 66205

913.384.3114

CLIENT
Eilts Design
DESIGNER
Patrice Eilts
DESIGN FIRM
Eilts, Anderson & Tracy Design
MANUFACTURER
Constable Hodgins Printing
TYPESETTER
Spirit Wind Arts
Fred Stubenrauch

PATRICE EILTS   JAN TRACY
5638 HOLMES.KCMO 64110 816.444.1920

CLIENT
Patrice Eilts and Jan Tracy
DESIGNER
Patrice Eilts
Jan Tracy
DESIGN FIRM
Eilts, Anderson & Tracy Design
MANUFACTURER
Insty Prints
TYPESETTER
Spirit Wind Arts
ILLUSTRATOR
Patrice Eilts

LITIGATION VIDEO

NORM LARSEN - PRESIDENT

2503 W. FRANKLIN AVE.

MPLS. MN. 55405-2323

PHONE - 612-374-5649

TELEFAX - 612-374-5049

CLIENT
Litigation Video
DESIGNER
Todd Hauswirth
DESIGN FIRM
C.S. Anderson Design Company
ILLUSTRATOR
Todd Hauswirth
TYPESETTER
Todd Hauswirth

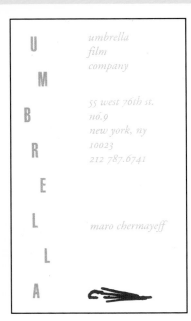

umbrella
film
company

55 west 76th st.
no.9
new york, ny
10023
212 787.6741

maro chermayeff

CLIENT
Umbrella Film Company
DESIGNER
Ivan Chermayeff
© Maro Chermayeff
DESIGN FIRM
Chermayeff & Geismar Inc.
PRINTER
Anchor Engraver

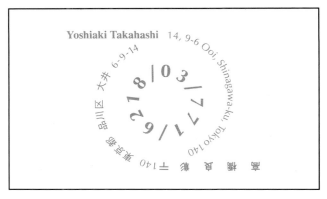

CLIENT
Yoshiaki Takahashi
DESIGNER
Andrew Serbinski
DESIGN FIRM
MACHINEART

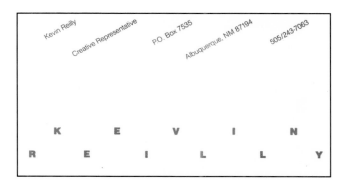

CLIENT
Kevin Reilly
DESIGNER
Steve Wedeen
DESIGN FIRM
Vaughn/Wedeen Creative
PRINTER
Academy Printing

CLIENT
Splash
ART DIRECTOR
Rita & Morgan Daly
DESIGNER
Rita & Morgan Daly
DESIGN FIRM
Daly & Daly Inc.
MANUFACTURER
Reynolds Dewalt Printing Inc.
TYPESETTER
Don Dewsnap Typographers

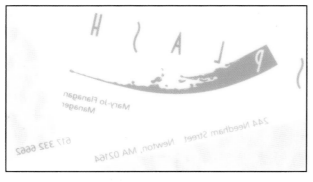

Peter de Sibour

201 584 0997

CLIENT
Peter de Sibour
DESIGNER
Peter de Sibour
DESIGN FIRM
Peter de Sibour de Sign
TYPESETTER
Peter de Sibour

CLIENT
Ellen Swandiak
DESIGNER
Ellen Swandiak
DESIGN FIRM
Swandiak Design
TYPESETTER
Elizabeth Type

CLIENT
Mary Matthews Interiors, Inc.
DESIGNER
Douglas Davie
Liisa Lindholm
DESIGN FIRM
Davie and Lindholm Design
Partnership
MANUFACTURER
Lithoprint
ILLUSTRATOR
Douglas Davie
Liisa Lindholm

Mary Matthews
President

Mary Matthews
Interiors Inc
1010 Franklin Ave
Garden City
New York 11530
Tel 516 747-2700
Fax 516 746-0941

CLIENT
Shirley Goodman Resource Center
DESIGNER
Takaaki Matsumoto
DESIGN FIRM
M Plus M Incorporated
MANUFACTURER
Monarch Press
TYPESETTER
M Plus M Incorporated

Barbara Castle
Assistant to the Executive Director

Shirley Goodman Resource Center
Fashion Institute of Technology

Seventh Avenue at 27th Street New York, NY 10001-5992
Telephone 212.760.7970 Facsimile 212.760.7978

The Riordan Foundation

Jill Riordan,
Chairman

300 South Grand Avenue
Twenty-Ninth Floor
Los Angeles, California 90071
213.229.8444

CLIENT
The Riordan Foundation
ART DIRECTOR
John Coy
DESIGNER
Sean Alatorre
Tom Bouman
DESIGN FIRM
COY, Los Angeles
MANUFACTURER
The Paper Blizzard
DESIGN AWARDS
Communication Arts 1989/90
Washington Trademark Association
1989/90

CLIENT
Martine Bruel Design
DESIGNER
Martine Bruel
DESIGN FIRM
Martine Bruel Design
MANUFACTURER
Alpha Press
TYPESETTER
Hamilton Phototype

MARTIN
E BRUEL
DESIGN

Martine Bruel Design
77 Martin Street, Cambridge, MA 02138
Tel & FAX 617/354/6714

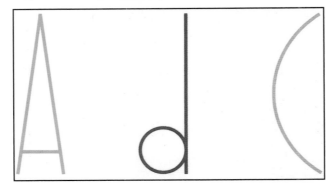

CLIENT
Aolia Donna Conrad
DESIGNER
Liz Rotter
DESIGN FIRM
Clifford Selbert Design
PRINTER
Aldus Press
TYPESETTER
Aolia Donna Conrad
DESIGN AWARDS
Hatch Awards

A. D. Conrad   3 Field Road   TEL 617 862 2207

Lexington MA   FAX 617 861 6102

02173

CLIENT
The AG Group
DESIGNER
John Jamieson
DESIGN FIRM
Designwerks!
PRINTER
Concord Graphic Arts
TYPESETTER
Brooks Typography

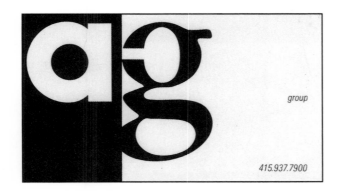

CLIENT
Arnold Zann Photography
DESIGNER
Jacklin Pinsler
DESIGN FIRM
Crosby Associates Inc.
TYPESETTER
Master Typographers

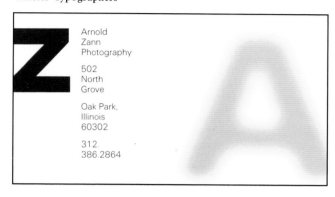

Arnold
Zann
Photography

502
North
Grove

Oak Park,
Illinois
60302

312.
386.2864

Bethlyn Vendryes
Project Director

200 Park Avenue South • New York, NY 10003 • 212 477 9005 • FAX 477 9006

CLIENT
D-ZINE, Inc.
DESIGNER
Bethlyn Vendryes
Linda Pierro
DESIGN FIRM
D-ZINE, Inc.
PRINTER
Sailsman Graphics

Bethlyn Vendryes
Project Director

34 West 15th Street
New York, NY 10011
212 691 6700

FAX 212 691 7151

Card Groups

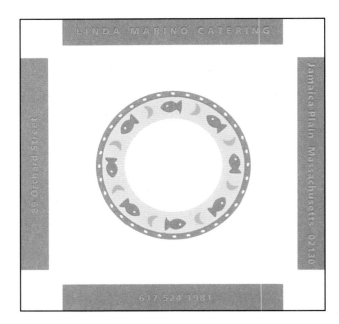

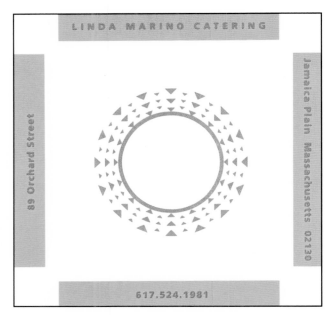

CLIENT
Linda Marino Catering
DESIGNER
Anita Meyer
DESIGN FIRM
plus design inc.
PRINTER
Aldus Press
ILLUSTRATOR
Anita Meyer
TYPESETTER
Monotype Composition Company
DESIGN AWARDS
A Decade of Type
Print Magazine/Regional
Design Award
Kudos From Hopper International
Design Competition

RUBY SHOES STUDIO

GRAPHIC COMMUNICATION

124 WATERTOWN STREET

WATERTOWN, MA 02172

P 617.923.9769

F 617.923.9826

ED HAUBEN
VP/EXECUTIVE DIRECTOR

RUBY SHOES STUDIO

GRAPHIC COMMUNICATION

124 WATERTOWN STREET

WATERTOWN, MA 02172

P 617.923.9769

F 617.923.9826

SUSAN TYRRELL
PRESIDENT/CREATIVE DIRECTOR

RUBY SHOES STUDIO

GRAPHIC COMMUNICATION

124 WATERTOWN STREET

WATERTOWN, MA 02172

P 617.923.9769

F 617.923.9826

DEB CAKE
PRODUCTION MANAGER

CLIENT
Ruby Shoes Studio
DESIGNER
Susan Tyrrell
Lisa Smith
Jane Lee
DESIGN FIRM
Ruby Shoes Studio
ILLUSTRATOR
Susan Tyrrell

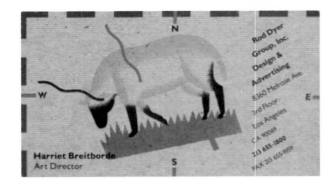

Harriet Breitborde
Art Director

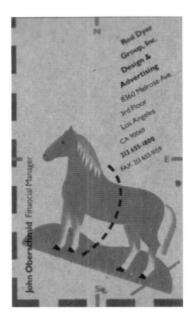

John Oberschmid Financial Manager

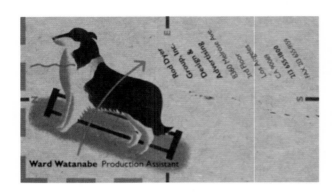

Ward Watanabe Production Assistant

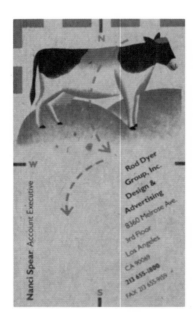

Nanci Spear Account Executive

Penny Howarth Art Director

CLIENT
Rod Dyer Group, Inc.
DESIGNER
Steve Twigger
DESIGN FIRM
Rod Dyer Group, Inc.
PRINTER
Anderson Printing
ILLUSTRATOR
Paul Leith

Rod Dyer President

CLIENT
Design Squad
ART DIRECTOR
Gail Rigelhaupt
Tom Dolle
DESIGNER
Gail Rigelhaupt
DESIGN FIRM
Design Squad

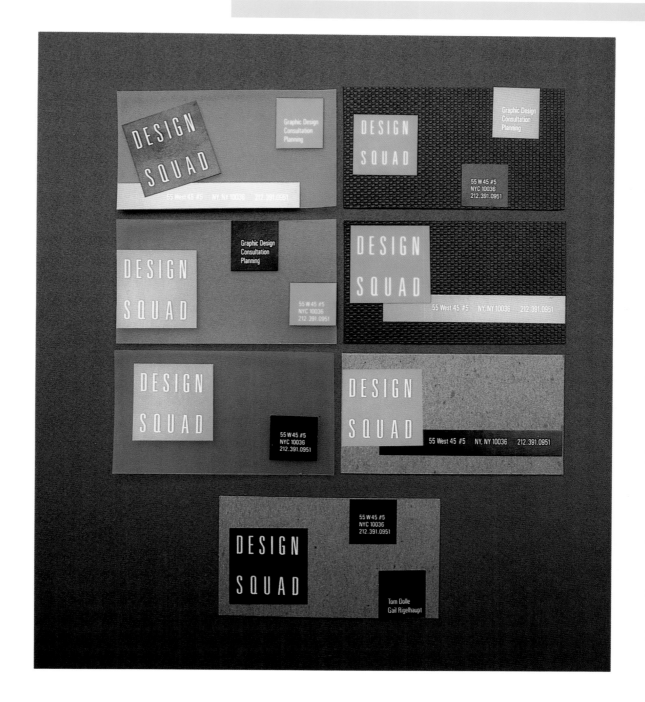

THOMAS DAIR
EXECUTIVE VICE PRESIDENT

SMART DESIGN inc.
7 WEST 18TH STREET
NEW YORK, NEW YORK 10011
TELEPHONE: 1 212 807 8150
FAX: 1 212 243 8514

STEPHEN RUSSAK

SMART DESIGN inc.
7 WEST 18TH STREET
NEW YORK, NEW YORK 10011
TELEPHONE: 1 212 807 8150
FAX: 1 212 243 8514

TAMARA THOMSEN
VICE PRESIDENT, GRAPHIC DESIGN

SMART DESIGN inc.
7 WEST 18TH STREET
NEW YORK, NEW YORK 10011
TELEPHONE: 1 212 807 8150
FAX: 1 212 243 8514

EVELYN TEPLOFF

SMART DESIGN inc.
7 WEST 18TH STREET
NEW YORK, NEW YORK 10011
TELEPHONE: 1 212 807 8150
FAX: 1 212 243 8514

CLIENT
Smart Design Inc.
ART DIRECTOR
Tamara Thomsen
DESIGNER
Laura Genninger
DESIGN FIRM
Smart Design Inc.
DESIGN AWARDS
GRAPHIS

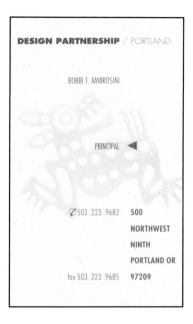

DESIGN PARTNERSHIP / PORTLAND

BOBBI T. AMBROSINI

PRINCIPAL ◄

503 .223 .9682 **500**

NORTHWEST

NINTH

PORTLAND OR

fax 503 .223 .9685 **97209**

DESIGN PARTNERSHIP / PORTLAND

RICHARD A. GOTTFRIED

PRINCIPAL ◄

503 .223 .9682 **500**

NORTHWEST

NINTH

PORTLAND OR

fax 503 .223 .9685 **97209**

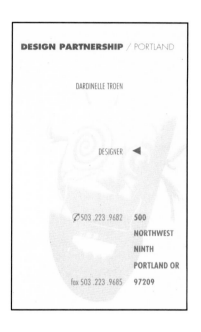

DESIGN PARTNERSHIP / PORTLAND

DARDINELLE TROEN

DESIGNER ◄

503 .223 .9682 **500**

NORTHWEST

NINTH

PORTLAND OR

fax 503 .223 .9685 **97209**

CLIENT
Design Partnership/Portland
DESIGNER
Kenneth G. Ambrosini
Dardinelle Troen
DESIGN FIRM
Design Partnership/Portland
PRINTER
Rose Press
TYPESETTER
In-house
ILLUSTRATOR
Resourced Art

CLIENT
Robin Thomas
Photographer
DESIGNER
Tucker Viemeister
DESIGN FIRM
Smart Design Inc.

ROBiN ThOMAS

Photographer

212-254-0271

CLIENT
No Dogs Design
DESIGNER
Robin Jareaux
DESIGN FIRM
No Dogs Design
MANUFACTURER
Concepts Unlimited
ILLUSTRATOR
Robin Jareaux
DESIGN AWARDS
Print **Regional Design Contest**

DESIGN

ERICH ROSE

Erich Rose
Designer

Edwin Schlossberg Inc
641 Sixth Avenue
New York NY 10011
Tel 212 989 3993
Fax 212 691 0290

DESIGN

Marc Beach
Systems Specialist

Edwin Schlossberg Inc
641 Sixth Avenue
New York NY 10011
Tel 212 989 3993
Fax 212 691 0290

DESIGN

Cynthia Caldora
Recruitment Coordinator

Edwin Schlossberg Inc
641 Sixth Avenue
New York NY 10011
Tel 212 989 3993
Fax 212 691 0290

DESIGN

John Branigan

Edwin Schlossberg Inc
641 Sixth Avenue
New York NY 10011
Tel 212 989 3993
Fax 212 691 0290

DESIGN

Michael Joyce
Senior Designer

Edwin Schlossberg Inc
641 Sixth Avenue
New York NY 10011
Tel 212 989 3993
Fax 212 691 0290

CLIENT
Edwin Schlossberg Incorporated
DESIGNER
Edwin Schlossberg
John Branigan
Joe Mayer
Andrew Proehl
DESIGN FIRM
Edwin Schlossberg Incorporated
© 1990 Edwin Schlossberg
Incorporated Business Cards
MANUFACTURER
Cosmo Litho

⚛ harris hart silver

Conscious Messages

51 west 16th street new york city 10011

THINK ABOUT IT

212 675 0273

CLIENT
Conscious Messages
DESIGNER
Gail Rigelhaupt
DESIGN FIRM
Rigelhaupt Design

CLIENT
Eymer Design
DESIGNER
Douglas + Selene Eymer
DESIGN FIRM
Eymer Design
PRINTER
The Smith Print
ILLUSTRATOR
Douglas Eymer
TYPESETTER
Berkeley Typography
DESIGN AWARDS
Print
HOW
DESI
Corporate ID
MACTAC

ARLENE BRADLEY

521 MADISON AVENUE
NEW YORK, NY 10022
TEL. 212-688-4450

ANTONIO SODDU

521 MADISON AVENUE
NEW YORK, NY 10022
TEL. 212-688-4450

MARIE SIGISMONDI

521 MADISON AVENUE
NEW YORK, NY 10022
TEL. 212-688-4450

CLIENT
The Spot
DESIGNER
Mike Quon
Eileen Kinneary
DESIGN FIRM
Mike Quon Design Office
DESIGN AWARDS
American Corporate Identity

CLIENT
Schaffer's Bridal Shop
DESIGNER
John Sayles
DESIGN FIRM
Sayles Graphic Design, Inc.
MANUFACTURER
Acme Printing Co.
ILLUSTRATOR
John Sayles
TYPESETTER
Printing Station

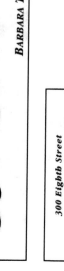

CLIENT
Ciro Design
DESIGNER
Joan Jung
DESIGN FIRM
Ciro Design
PRINTER
Commerce Printers

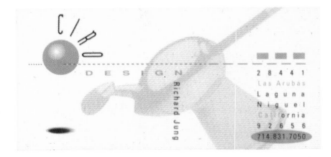

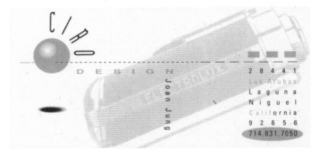

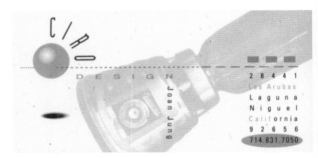

and Linda

THARP ∧ DID IT

FIFTY UNIVERSITY AVENUE

SUITE NUMBER TWENTY ONE

LOS GATOS, CALIFORNIA 95030

408.354.6726 • FAX 354.1450

SAN FRANCISCO 415.362.4494

RICK THARP
ART DIRECTOR·DESIGNER

THARP DID IT

FIFTY UNIVERSITY AVENUE

SUITE NUMBER TWENTY ONE

LOS GATOS, CALIFORNIA 95030

408.354.6726 • FAX 354.1450

SAN FRANCISCO 415.362.4494

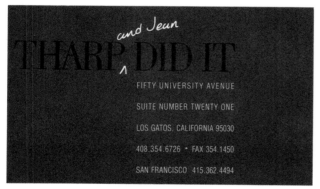

and Jean

THARP ∧ DID IT

FIFTY UNIVERSITY AVENUE

SUITE NUMBER TWENTY ONE

LOS GATOS, CALIFORNIA 95030

408.354.6726 • FAX 354.1450

SAN FRANCISCO 415.362.4494

LINDA WOODRUFF
DESIGN ADMINISTRATOR

CLIENT
THARP DID IT
DESIGNER
Acme Business Cards
DESIGN FIRM
THARP DID IT
MANUFACTURER
Acme Business Cards
PAPER
Simpson Evergreen
TYPESETTER
Acme Business Cards

Die-Cut & Embossed Cards

NJ Black & Compa...
Commercial
Real Estate
Services
Nicholas J. Black
20 First Plaza
Suite 515
Albuquerque
New Mexico 8710...

o-Facial Sur...

PLAZA

...M DESIGN, INC.
...H AVENUE
...RK 10011

...3020

...fax

BLACKSTONE RIVER VALLE...

Richard T. Kleber • National Park Ranger...

Post Office Box 730
15 Mendon Street
Uxbridge, MA 01569

R E M E M B E R   Y O U R   P L A...

...AMERI...

NYC's Famous XIX Hole

The British ...pe...

Where you don't have to keep your left arm stra...

Ken Z...
Project ...
602 · 2...

320 East 59th Street
New York, NY 10022
...55-9467

I PEZZI DIPINTI

CATHRYN COLLINS

...H STREET TOWNHOUSE 11
...NY 10021
...7-2997

Mike Arm...
3131 W. 18...
Torrance, CA...
213...

Celia Keywor...

Celia Key...
108 Torri...
London NW5...
Telephone 071 267 0...
...071 482 1426

POD DESI...

Amy Stucke
318 E. Hadley
...ayton, Ohio
...419
...2353

SHELLEY DANYS...

Gra...

S T U D I O

BARBARA FELDMA...

421 N. Rod...
Suite
Bever...
Califo...
213/ART 44...

Iris Bell
graphic design
• • • • • • • •
333 East 49 Str...
New York, NY...
2 1 2 · 7 5 1 ...

CLIENT
Mike Armijo Design Office
DESIGNER
Mike Armijo
DESIGN FIRM
Mike Armijo Design Office
TYPESETTER
Composition Type
ILLUSTRATOR
Mike Armijo

TOM DUFFY

CAFE TOMA
371 11TH STREET
SAN FRANCISCO, CALIFO
ORNIA 94103
PHONE 252.5320
FAX 252.5322

CLIENT
Cafe Toma
DESIGNER
Bruce Yelaska
DESIGN FIRM
Bruce Yelaska Design
MANUFACTURER
Vision Printing
TYPESETTER
CityType
DESIGN AWARDS
American Corporate Identity

NYC's Famous XIX Hole

The British Open

Where you don't have to keep your left arm straight.

320 East 59th Street
New York, NY 10022
212.355.8467

CLIENT
The British Open
DESIGNER
Stephen M. McAllister
DESIGN FIRM
Design Matters
TYPESETTER
Design Matters
DESIGN AWARDS
DESI Award
1992 *Graphic Design:USA*

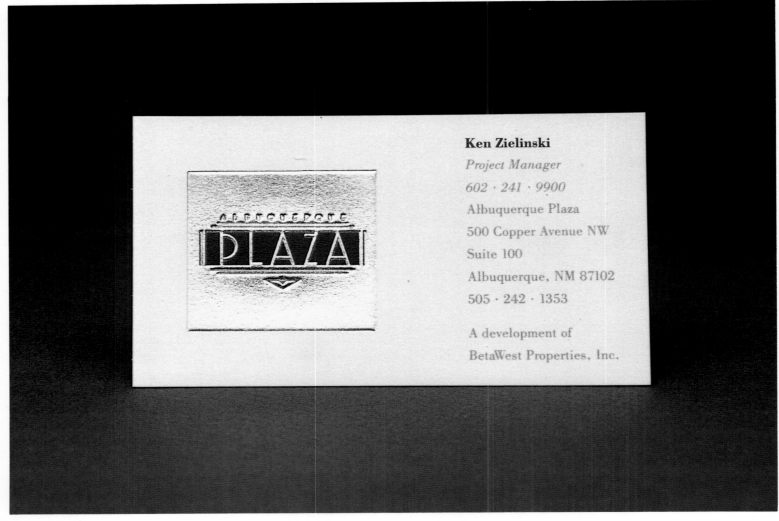

Ken Zielinski

Project Manager

602 · 241 · 9900

Albuquerque Plaza

500 Copper Avenue NW

Suite 100

Albuquerque, NM 87102

505 · 242 · 1353

A development of

BetaWest Properties, Inc.

CLIENT
Albuquerque Plaza
DESIGNER
Rick Vaughn
Steve Wedeen
DESIGN FIRM
Vaughn/Wedeen Creative
PRINTER
Albuquerque Printing
DESIGN AWARDS
Local Addy Award

LUTEN
CLAREY
STERN

Luten Clarey Stern

Corporation

1059 Third Avenue

New York City 10021

212-838-6420

Fax 212-751-6457

CLIENT
Luten Clarey Stern
DESIGNER
Tyler Smith
DESIGN FIRM
Tyler Smith Design
TYPESETTER
TM Productions

DOUG NIXON

PRINT

2930 McGEE
TRAFFICWAY
KCMO 64108
816 842 6101

CLIENT
Nic Print Printing
DESIGNER
Patrice Eilts
DESIGN FIRM
Eilts, Anderson & Tracy Design
MANUFACTURER
Nic Print
TYPESETTER
Lopez Graphics
DESIGN AWARDS
A Decade of Type
PIE *Business Stationery*
Zanders Paper Awards
Gold—local Addy Awards

THE LARRY McADAMS
GROUP

MARKETING • ADVERTISING • DESIGN

LARRY McADAMS
PRESIDENT
▲

1400 BRISTOL ST. N.
SUITE 220 • NEWPORT
BEACH • CALIF. 92660
PH. (714) 833-8333
FAX (714) 833-1083

CLIENT
The Larry McAdams Group
DESIGNER
Larry McAdams
DESIGN FIRM
The McAdams Group
PRINTER
Burdge, Inc.
ILLUSTRATOR
Larry McAdams
TYPESETTER
Page One

CLIENT
Perfect Touch
DESIGNER
Peter Lord
TYPESETTER
Macintosh

CLIENT
Larry Vigon Studio
ART DIRECTOR
Larry Vigon
DESIGNERS
Larry Vigon
Brian Jackson
DESIGN FIRM
Larry Vigon Studio
ILLUSTRATOR
Larry Vigon

CLIENT
Barbara Feldman
ART DIRECTOR
Larry Vigon
DESIGNERS
Larry Vigon
Brian Jackson
DESIGN FIRM
Larry Vigon Studio
MANUFACTURER
Anderson

CLIENT
Celia Keyworth
DESIGNER
John Rushworth
DESIGN FIRM
Pentagram Design Ltd.
MANUFACTURER
Croft Printers

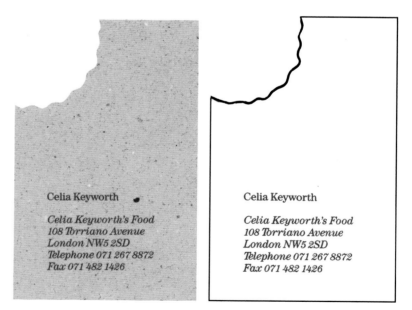

CLIENT
Milwaukee Sound Studios
DESIGNER
Steve Quinn
DESIGN FIRM
Quinn Design
PRINTER
Classic Impressions
TYPESETTER
Macintosh

CLIENT
Manlove Photography
Joe Manlove
DESIGNER
Tony Ross
DESIGN FIRM
Ross Design Inc.
ILLUSTRATOR
John Francis
TYPESETTER
Macintosh
DESIGN AWARDS
Addy Award of Delaware

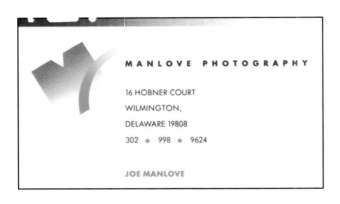

CLIENT
Notovitz Design Inc.
DESIGNER
Gil Livne
DESIGN FIRM
Notovitz Design Inc.
MANUFACTURER
Karr Graphics Corp.
DESIGN AWARDS
Neena Paper
Rockport Publishing

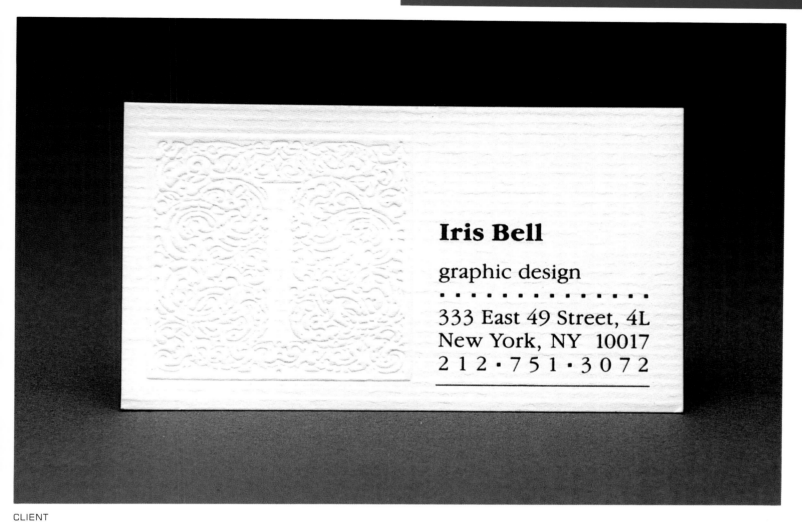

CLIENT
Iris Bell
DESIGNER
Iris Bell
DESIGN FIRM
Iris Bell
MANUFACTURER
Mainline Thermographers
TYPESETTER
Bill Platske

Carl Johnson

Certified Public Accountant
747 Pontiac Avenue
Cranston, RI 02910-5824

401-781-7775   *Carl C. Johnson, CPA*

CLIENT
Carl Johnson, CPA
DESIGNER
Tim Claflin
DESIGN FIRM
Tim Claflin Design
TYPESETTER
Typesetting Service
DESIGN AWARDS
R.I. Supershow-1st.
Corporate Communications

1400 Oak Avenue

St. Helena, California

94574

phone ~ 707 ~ 963 ~ 3115

fax ~ 707 ~ 963 ~ 3121

SALLY TANTAU ~ MARGO TANTAU

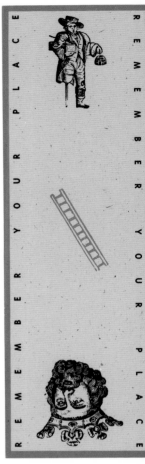

CLIENT
Tantau
DESIGNER
Cary Michael Trout
DESIGN FIRM
Trout & Trout
TYPESETTER
Macintosh/Andresen Typographics
ILLUSTRATOR
Cary Trout

CLIENT
Bob Aufuldish
DESIGNER
Bob Aufuldish
DESIGN FIRM
Aufuldish & Warinner
PRINTER
Logos Graphics
TYPESETTER
A & W

CLIENT
Shelley Danysh
DESIGNER
Shelley Danysh
DESIGN FIRM
Shelley Danysh Studio
TYPESETTER
L & B Typo

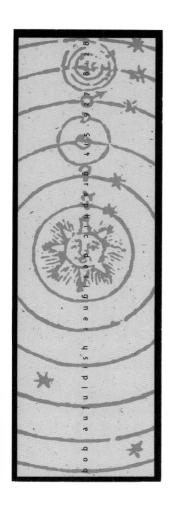

Richard T. Kleber • National Park Ranger

Post Office Box 730
15 Mendon Street
Uxbridge, MA 01569
Tel 508 278 · 9400
Fax 508 278 · 3516

CLIENT
Blackstone River Valley
DESIGNER
Melanie Lowe
DESIGN FIRM
Clifford Selbert Design
PRINTER
United Lithograph
TYPESETTER
Clifford Selbert Design

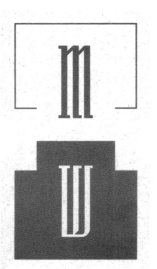

design M design W

James Westhall

22 second street
troy, ny 12180

518.273.5994
fx/md 518.273.6106

CLIENT
design M design W
DESIGNER
Maureen Maloney
James Westhall
DESIGN FIRM
design M design W
MANUFACTURER
Chase Thermographers
DESIGN AWARDS
NORI, American Catalog Awards

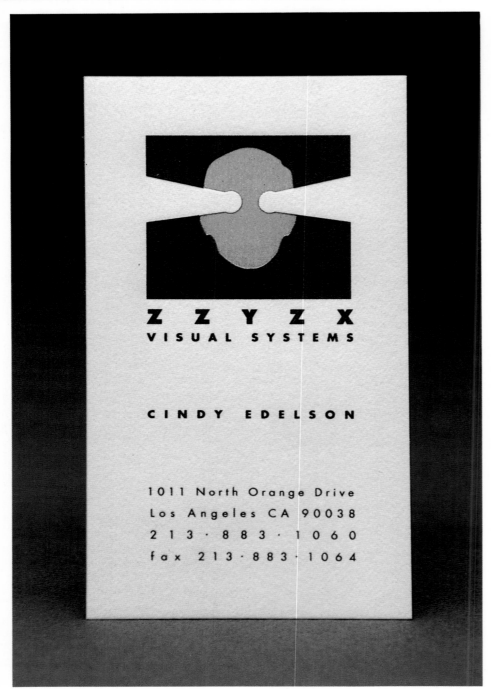

CLIENT
ZZYZX
ART DIRECTOR
Larry Vigon
DESIGNERS
Larry Vigon
Brian Jackson
DESIGN FIRM
Larry Vigon Studio

NJ Black & Company
Commercial
Real Estate
Services
Nicholas J. Black
20 First Plaza
Suite 515
Albuquerque
New Mexico 87102
505/242-2885

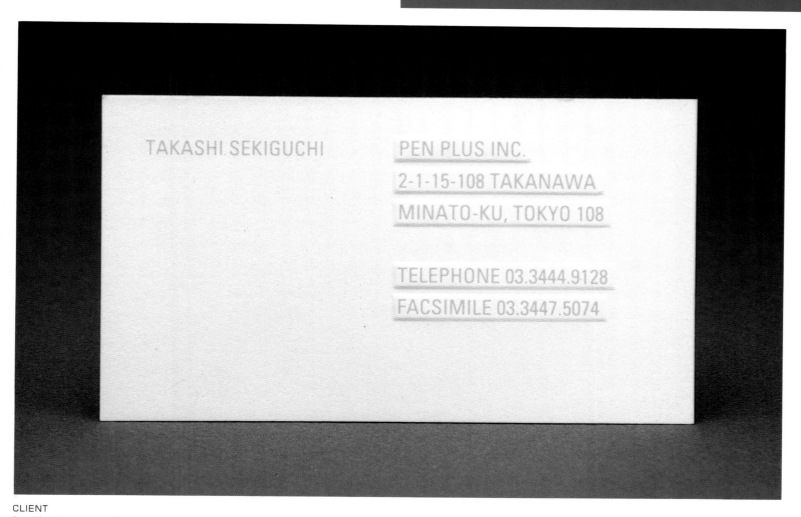

CLIENT
Pen Plus Incorporated
DESIGNER
Takaaki Matsumoto
DESIGN FIRM
M Plus M Incorporated
MANUFACTURER
Continental- Burnique Ltd.
TYPESETTER
M Plus M Incorporated

CLIENT
NJ Black & Company
DESIGNER
Steve Wedeen
DESIGN FIRM
Vaughn/Wedeen Creative
PRINTER
Academy Printers
TYPESETTERS
Typesavers

CLIENT
GVO
DESIGNER
Jay Wilson
DESIGN FIRM
GVO Inc.
MANUFACTURER
Neilsen Printing
TYPESETTER
Scott Peterson Graphic Services

S O N S O L E S
L L O R E N S

Pg. de Sant Joan 36 pral. 1º
08010 Barcelona. Fax 265 92 84
Tels. 246 45 79 - 265 92 84

CLIENT
Sonsoles Llorens
DESIGNER
Sonsoles Llorens
DESIGN FIRM
Sonsoles Llorens
MANUFACTURER
Barguñó y Cia

NATIONAL
MOWER REPAIR

551 MAIN AVENUE
WALLINGTON, N.J. 07057
2 0 1 – 6 1 4 – 0 0 1 0
8 0 0 – 8 7 3 – 7 3 7 2

CLIENT
National Mower Repair
DESIGNER
Schlesinger/Quinn
DESIGN FIRM
Platinum Design
MANUFACTURER
Issacson
TYPESETTER
Tribecca Typographers

I PEZZI DIPINTI

CATHRYN COLLINS

333 EAST 69TH STREET TOWNHOUSE 11
NEW YORK, NY 10021
TELEPHONE 212.737.2997
FACSIMILE 212.650.0092

CLIENT
I Pezzi DiPinti
DESIGNER
Takaaki Matsumoto
DESIGN FIRM
M Plus M Incorporated
TYPESETTER
M Plus M Incorporated

CLIENT
Tokyo Tower Development Co.
DESIGNER
April Greiman
DESIGN FIRM
April Greiman Inc.
MANUFACTURER
Monarch Litho

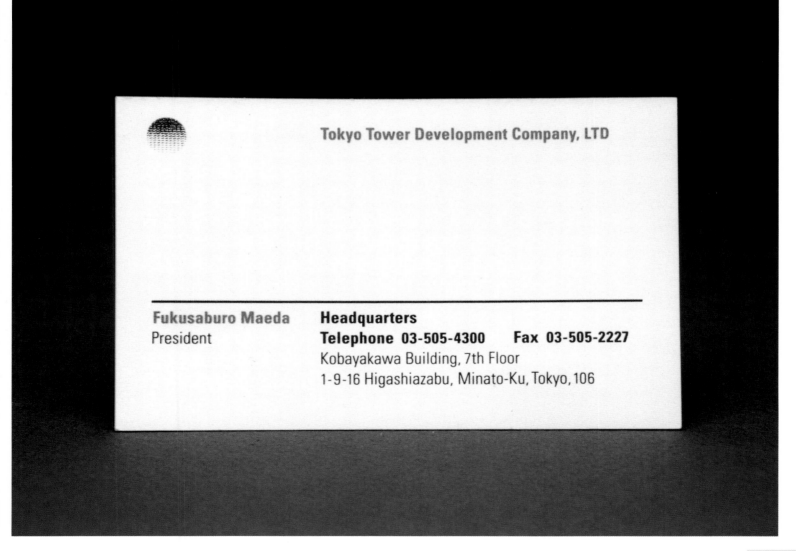

CLIENT
Savoy
DESIGNER
Julie Salestrom
Linda Zingg
DESIGN FIRM
Salestrom Design, Inc.
MANUFACTURER
Lehman Brothers
TYPESETTER
Macintosh
ILLUSTRATOR
Julie Salestrom
Linda Zingg

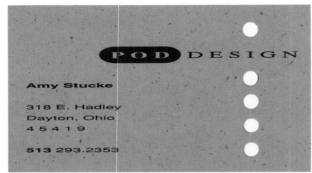

CLIENT
Pod Design
DESIGNER
Amy Stucke
DESIGN FIRM
Pod Design

CLIENT
Spot Design
DESIGNER
J. Drew Hodges
DESIGN FIRM
Spot Design

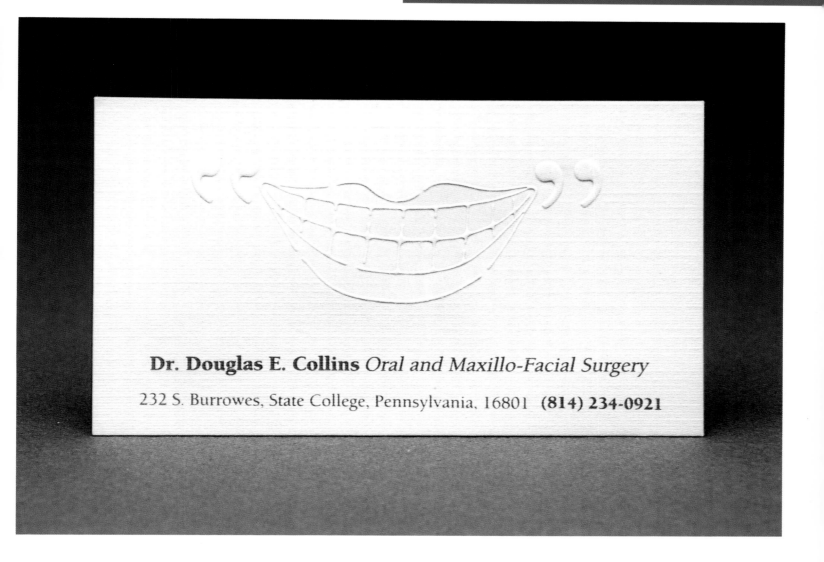

Dr. Douglas E. Collins *Oral and Maxillo-Facial Surgery*

232 S. Burrowes, State College, Pennsylvania, 16801 **(814) 234-0921**

CLIENT
Dr. Douglas E. Collins
DESIGNER
Lanny Sommese
DESIGN FIRM
Sommese Design
MANUFACTURER
Nittany Valley Offset
ILLUSTRATOR
Lanny Sommese

Special Sizes & Construction

SEYMOUR ROBINS DESIGN
*". . . making thought visible
and vision thoughtful."*

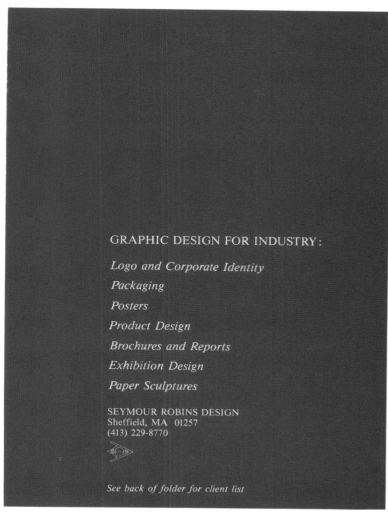

GRAPHIC DESIGN FOR INDUSTRY:

Logo and Corporate Identity

Packaging

Posters

Product Design

Brochures and Reports

Exhibition Design

Paper Sculptures

SEYMOUR ROBINS DESIGN
Sheffield, MA 01257
(413) 229-8770

See back of folder for client list

CLIENT
Seymour Robins Design
DESIGNER
Seymour Robins
DESIGN FIRM
Seymour Robins Design
MANUFACTURER
The Pond-Ekberg Co.
TYPESETTER
The Pond-Ekberg Co.

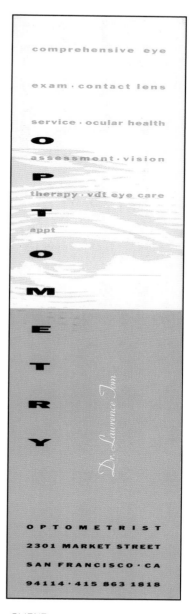

CLIENT
Urban Eyes
DESIGNER
Alan Disparte
Timothy Harris
DESIGN FIRM
Timothy Harris Design
TYPESETTER
Petro Graphics
ILLUSTRATOR
Alan Disparte
Timothy Harris

CLIENT
Salestrom Design, Inc.
DESIGNER
Julie Salestrom
DESIGN FIRM
Salestrom Design, Inc.
MANUFACTURER
Gramercy Offset
TYPESETTER
Macintosh
ILLUSTRATOR
Julie Salestrom

CLIENT
Barnstorming Designs
DESIGNER
Teddie Barnhart
DESIGN FIRM
Barnstorming Designs
© 1987
MANUFACTURER
Self/ Rubber Stamps
ILLUSTRATOR
Teddie Barnhart
TYPESETTER
Typestyle
DESIGN AWARDS
Print's Regional Design Annual

CLIENT
Bill Phelps
DESIGNER
Haley Johnson
DESIGN FIRM
C.S. Anderson Design Company
TYPESETTER
Haley Johnson
DESIGN AWARDS
AIGA 1 Color & 2 Color 1992
AIGA Minnesota 1992
ID **Magazine 1992**

John Davies

PO Box 1220 Grand Cayman British West Indies Telephone 809 94 95758 Telex 4392 Fax 809 94 97707 IMAGE

CLIENT
John Davies
DESIGNER
John Rushworth
DESIGN FIRM
Pentagram Design Ltd.
MANUFACTURER
Gavin Martin Ltd.
ILLUSTRATOR
Frank Schöeder

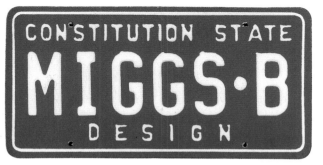

CLIENT
Miggs B Design
DESIGNER
Miggs Burroughs
DESIGN FIRM
Miggs B Design
MANUFACTURER
**Printing and thermography by
Banner Press
Embossing by Eccles Engraving**

147 Fern Street
Hartford
Connecticut 06105

Ostro Design

Telephone
203-231-9698
Facsimile
203-231-9602

CLIENT
Ostro Design
DESIGNER
Michael Ostro
DESIGN FIRM
Ostro Design
MANUFACTURER
Briarwood Printing Co./Swanson Engraving
TYPESETTER
Mono Typesetting Co.
DESIGN AWARDS
1992 American Center For Design/100 Show
1991 AIGA/Just Type Two
1991 Connecticut Art Directors Club
1991 Print Regional Design Annual

...For the Spirit
...For the Mind
...For the Body
...For the Skin You are In !

For the ultimate escape
to an environment of
detoxification, rejuvenation
relaxation & indulgence.

We offer an impressive array
of methods and services
to give you an exquisite
complexion that will make
you more desirable.

To experience this great escape,
take an hour for yourself
or an entire day.

For more information Call
302-652-8000

The Plaza
1303 Delaware Avenue
Wilmington, Delaware 19806

ZOHRA
SPA & CLINIQUE

CLIENT
Zohra Spa & Clinique
DESIGNER
Tony Ross
DESIGN FIRM
Ross Design Inc.
ILLUSTRATOR
Conrad Velasco
TYPESETTER
Macintosh
DESIGN AWARDS
Print **Magazine**
Adde Award

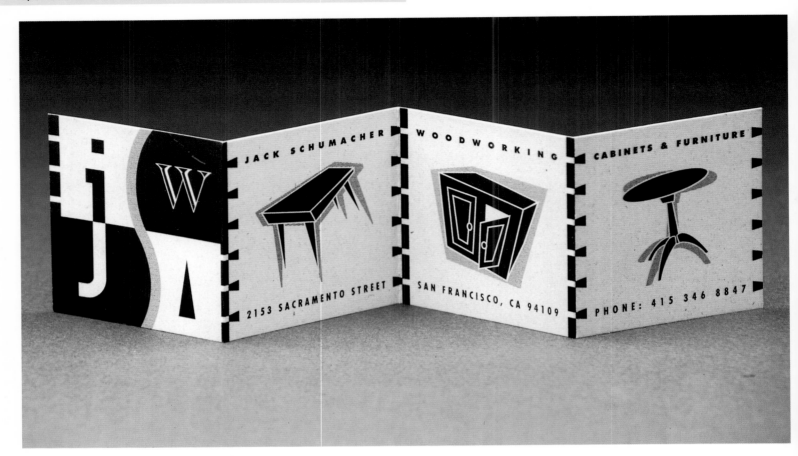

CLIENT
Jack Schumarcher Woodworking
DESIGNER
Christine McFarren
MANUFACTURER
At Printing
ILLUSTRATOR
Christine McFarren
TYPESETTER
Macintosh

CLIENT
Eurocare
Chris Marganski
DESIGNER
Joanne & Ed Rebek
DESIGN FIRM
JOED Design

CHRIS MARGANSKI
708·687·8289

EURO
CARE

PERSONALIZED CARE
FOR YOUR EUROPEAN
AUTOMOBILE

• GUARANTEED SERVICE

• FACTORY TRAINED
PORSCHE, AUDI, VW
MERCEDES BENZ

• FREE PICK-UP AND DELIVERY

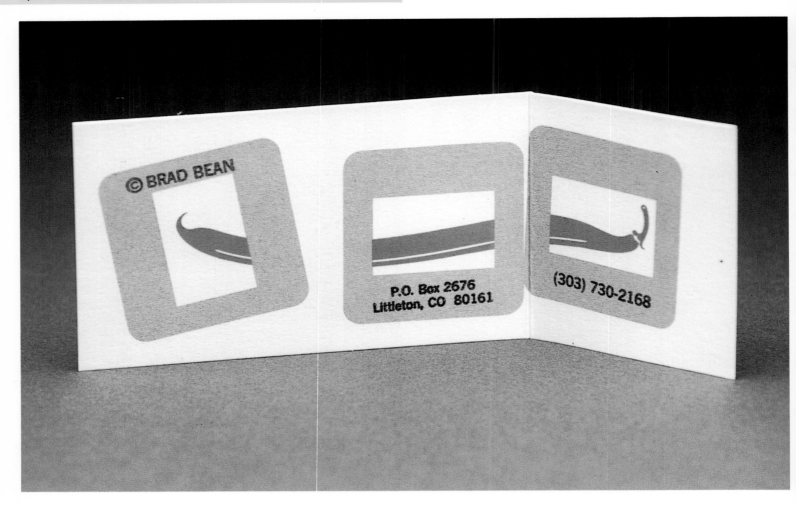

CLIENT
Brad Bean
DESIGNER
Don Weller
DESIGN FIRM
The Weller Institute for the
Cure of Design, Inc.
MANUFACTURER
Graphic Reproductions
ILLUSTRATOR
Don Weller
TYPESETTER
Whipple Inc.

CLIENT
Spontaneous Combustion
DESIGNER
Patrice Eilts
DESIGN FIRM
Eilts, Anderson & Tracy Design
MANUFACTURER
Insty Prints
TYPESETTER
Deidre Eilts
ILLUSTRATOR
Patrice Eilts
DESIGN AWARDS
Print Design Annual
1st Annual Print Logos
Gold—Kansas City Art Directors
PIE *International Logos*
A Decade of Type
Letterhead & Logo Design

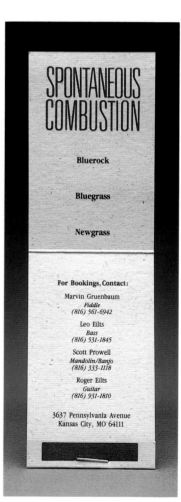

CLIENT
Clockwork Apple Inc.
DESIGNER
Christo Holloway
DESIGN ASSISTANT
Aryeh Hecht of Visual Persuasion
DESIGN FIRM
Clockwork Apple Inc.
PRINTING
Graphic Impressions
STAINLESS STEEL ETCHING
Insight Design

Clockwork Apple Inc.
57 Laight St. Suite 1
New York NY 10013
Tel (212) 431-8996
Fax (212) 226-4906

Christo Holloway

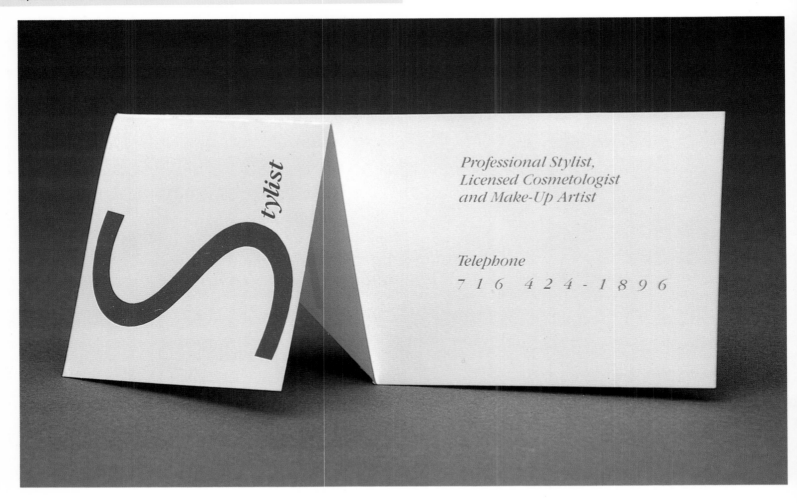

CLIENT
Susan J. Tontarshi
DESIGNER
James Selak
DESIGN FIRM
James L. Selak Design
MANUFACTURER
Ayer & Streb, Inc.
TYPESETTER
Rochester Monotype
DESIGN AWARDS
Print Casebooks

CLIENT
The Magic of Salvatore
DESIGNER
Carole Brodkin
DESIGN FIRM
Brodkin & Associates
TYPESETTER
Armstrong Graphic Services
ILLUSTRATOR
Carole Brodkin

CLIENT
**Loebl Schlossman and Hackl
Architects**
DESIGNER
Rick Eiber
DESIGN FIRM
Rick Eiber Design (RED)
MANUFACTURER
Rohner Printing
TYPESETTER
The Type Gallery, Inc.

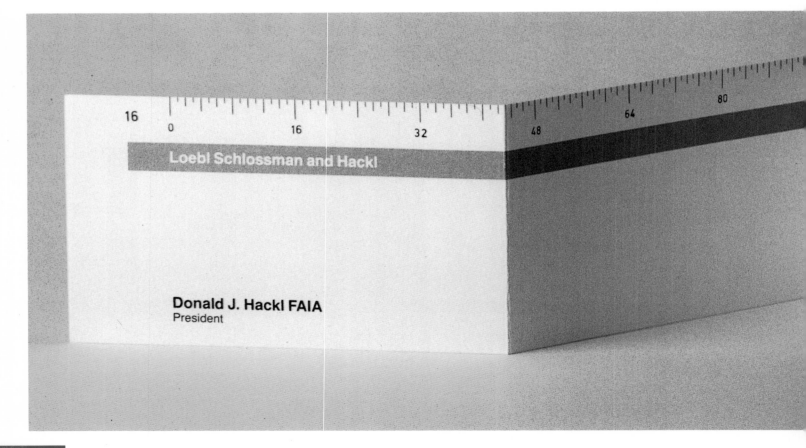

R E D ■

Nadine Hajjar

Red Square Design
150 West 11 Street
New York, N.Y. 10011
212 675 6442

CLIENT
Red Square Design
DESIGNER
Lev Zeitlin
Nadine Hajjar
DESIGN FIRM
Red Square Design
TYPESETTER
Typogram

Sean Adams   213 660 7797

vivir mejor por diseño elegante y refinado   2130
Lyric Avenue
Los Angeles
California
90027

CLIENT
Sean Adams
DESIGNER
Sean Adams
DESIGN FIRM
Sean Adams
MANUFACTURER
Paper Blizzard

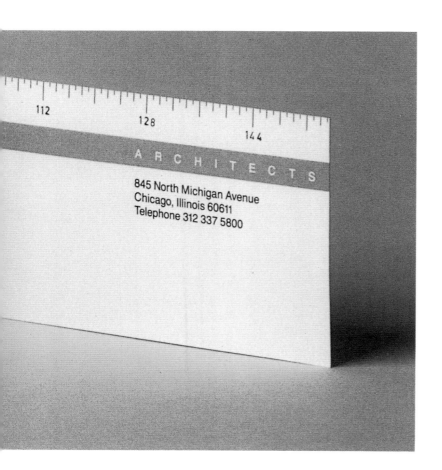

112   128   144
A R C H I T E C T S
845 North Michigan Avenue
Chicago, Illinois 60611
Telephone 312 337 5800

GRAPHIC
DESIGN
BUSINESS
CONSULTANT

EMILY RUTH COHEN

FOURTEEN
HURLEY AVENUE
NORTH PLAINFIELD
NEW JERSEY
07060

TELEPHONE/FAX
908.754.1326

CLIENT
Emily Ruth Cohen
DESIGNER
Ellen Lynch
DESIGN FIRM
Ellen Lynch
PRINTER
Lorshelle Printing

CLIENT
Platinum Design
DESIGNER
Schlesinger/Peslak
DESIGN FIRM
Platinum Design
PRINTER
Brodock Press

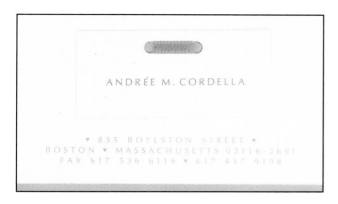

▼ 855 BOYLSTON STREET ▼
BOSTON ▼ MASSACHUSETTS 02116-2601
FAX 617 536 6119 ▼ 617 437 9198

CLIENT
Cordella Design
DESIGNER
Andree Cordella
DESIGN FIRM
Cordella Design
MANUFACTURER
Cordella Design
TYPESETTER
Typographic House
ENGRAVER
Adolph Bauer
DESIGN AWARDS
New York Art Directors
Hatch
Creative Club of Boston
AIGA

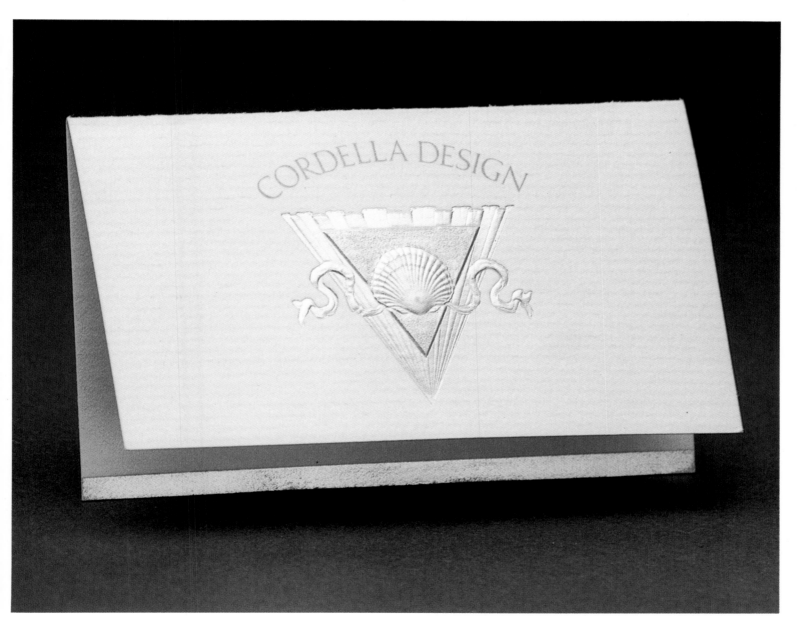

CLIENT
Jeffrey Coolidge Photography
DESIGNER
Douglas Eymer
DESIGN FIRM
Eymer Design
PRINTER
Alden Press
ILLUSTRATOR
Mark Fisher
Douglas Eymer
TYPESETTER
Berkeley Typographers
DESIGN AWARDS
AIGA
HOW
Print
Creative Club of Boston
DESI

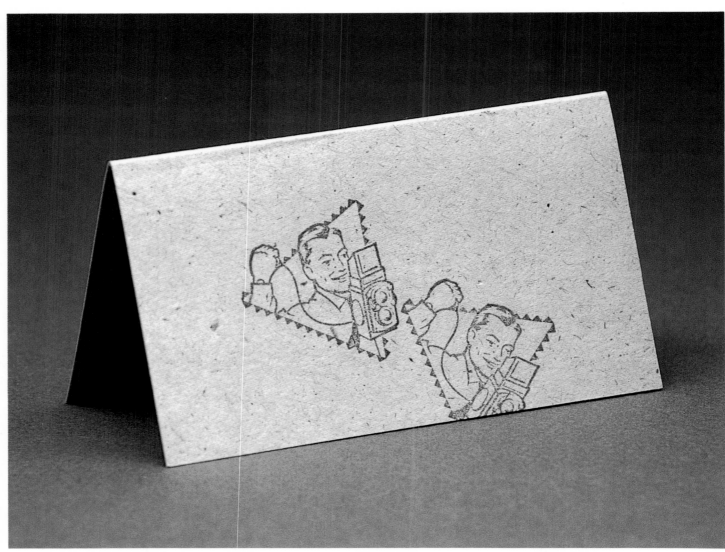

CLIENT
Dante's Restaurants, Inc.
DESIGNER
Lanny Sommese
DESIGN FIRM
Sommese Design
MANUFACTURER
Commercial Printing
ILLUSTRATOR
Lanny Sommese
TYPESETTER
Commercial Litho

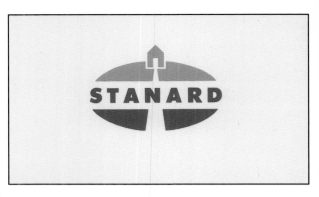

CLIENT
João Machado
DESIGNER
João Machado
DESIGN FIRM
João Machado
MANUFACTURER
Marca

CLIENT
The Stanard Realty Company
DESIGNER
Michael Stanard
DESIGN FIRM
Michael Stanard, Incorporated

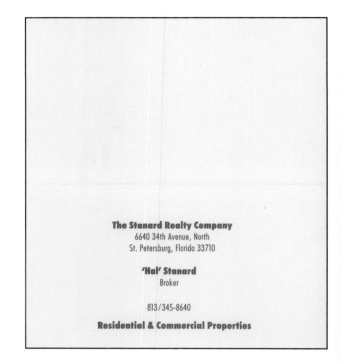

CLIENT
Kathy Warinner
DESIGNER
Kathy Warinner
DESIGN FIRM
Aufuldish & Warinner
PRINTER
Logos Graphics
ILLUSTRATOR
Kathy Warinner
TYPESETTER
A & W

Sharyn Yuen
36 Powell Street
2nd Floor
Vancouver, B.C. v6a 1e7
Canada
(604) 687-3296

Kakali

Handmade Papers

CLIENT
Kakali Handmade Papers
DESIGNER
Keith Martin
DESIGN FIRM
Studio Allsorts

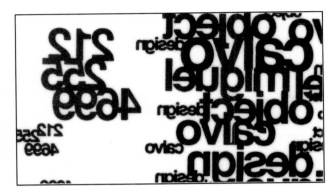

CLIENT
Calvo Object Design
DESIGNER
Miguel Calvo
DESIGN FIRM
Calvo Object Design
MANUFACTURER
Village Copier

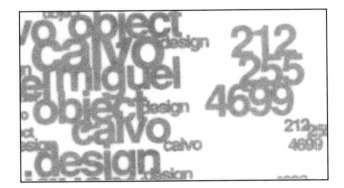

CLIENT
Good Pictures
DESIGNER
Jennifer Morla
Sharrie Brooks
DESIGN FIRM
Morla Design
MANUFACTURER
On Paper
TYPESETTER
Display Lettering

Jonathan Keeton

600 Townsend
Suite 321 West
San Francisco
CA 94103
415.621.1455
Fax 415.252.7212

CLIENT
Veen & Co.
DESIGNER
Elizabeth Bakacs
DESIGN FIRM
Manville Bakacs Santana
MANUFACTURER
Charlton & Charlton Lithographers

VEEN & CO.
399 Bleecker Street
New York, NY. 10014
212·727·3988

Lanny Sommese
Design and Illustration
481 Glenn Road
State College
Pennsylvania 16801
(814) 238-7484

CLIENT
Sommese Design
Professor Sommese
DESIGNER
Lanny Sommese
DESIGN FIRM
Sommese Design
MANUFACTURER
Grove Printing
ILLUSTRATOR
Lanny Sommese
TYPESETTER
Commercial Litho

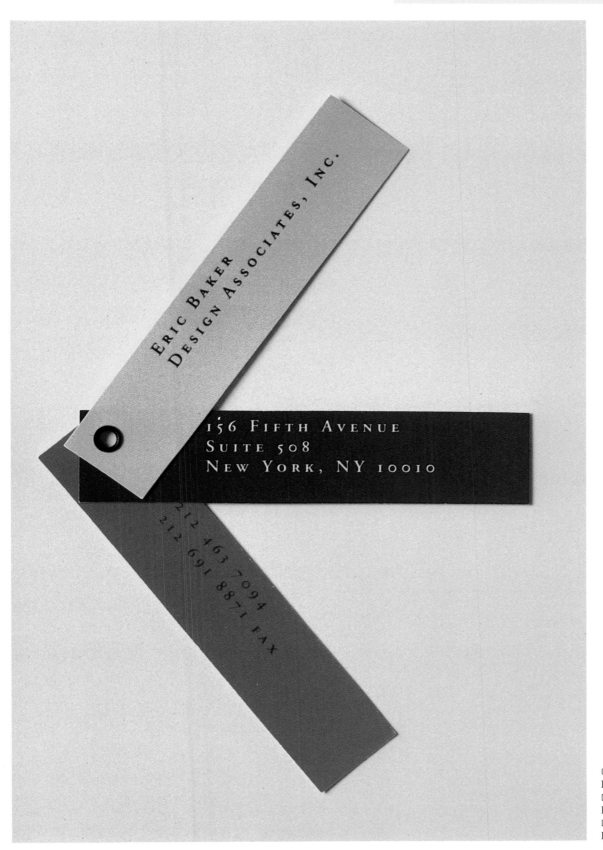

ERIC BAKER
DESIGN ASSOCIATES, INC.

156 FIFTH AVENUE
SUITE 508
NEW YORK, NY 10010

212 463 7094
212 691 8871 FAX

CLIENT
Eric Baker Design Associates, Inc.
DESIGNER
Eric Baker
DESIGN FIRM
Eric Baker Design Associates, Inc.

CLIENT
Sam A. Angeloff
DESIGNER
Rick Eiber
DESIGN FIRM
Rick Eiber Design (RED)
MANUFACTURER
Artcraft Printing Co.
TYPESETTER
The Type Gallery
DESIGN AWARDS
Gold—New York Art Directors Club

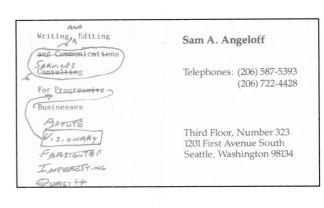

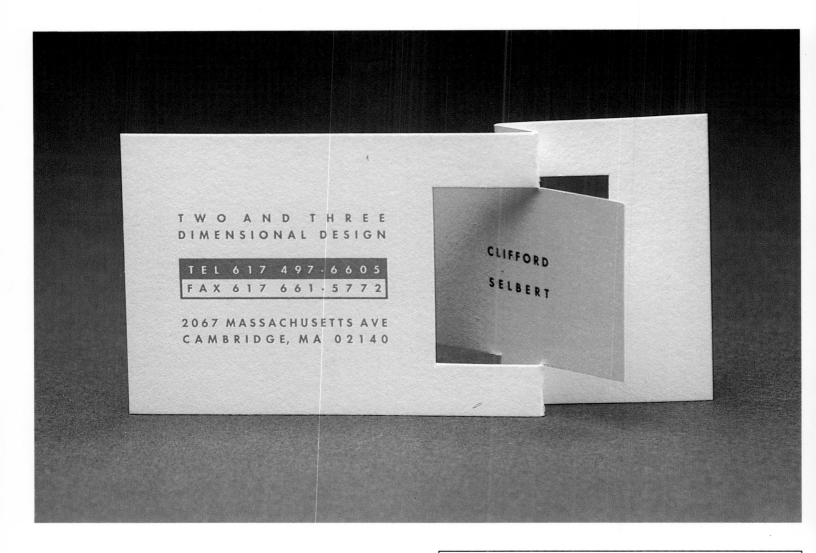

CLIENT
Clifford Selbert Design
DESIGNER
Melanie Lowe
DIE-CUT DESIGNER
Joyce Culkin
DESIGN FIRM
Clifford Selbert Design
TYPESETTER
Melanie Lowe

On the triangle:

Willa Scantlebury Advertising & Design

87 North Sussex St. & Rt. 46

Dover, NJ 07801 P 201-366-5700 F 201-366-7666

CLIENT
Willa Scantlebury
DESIGNER
Willa Scantlebury Advertising
& Design
DESIGN FIRM
Willa Scantlebury Advertising
& Design
TYPESETTER
New Type

CLIENT
Litigation Graphics
DESIGNER
Marsha Drebelbis
DESIGN FIRM
Marsha Drebelbis

CLIENT
Charly Brown + Co.
DESIGNER
Tom Bonauro
DESIGN FIRM
Tom Bonauro Design
MANUFACTURER
Logos Graphics

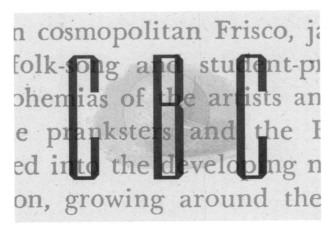

Charly Brown + Co
314 12th Street
San Francisco 94103
415-861-6084

Charly Brown

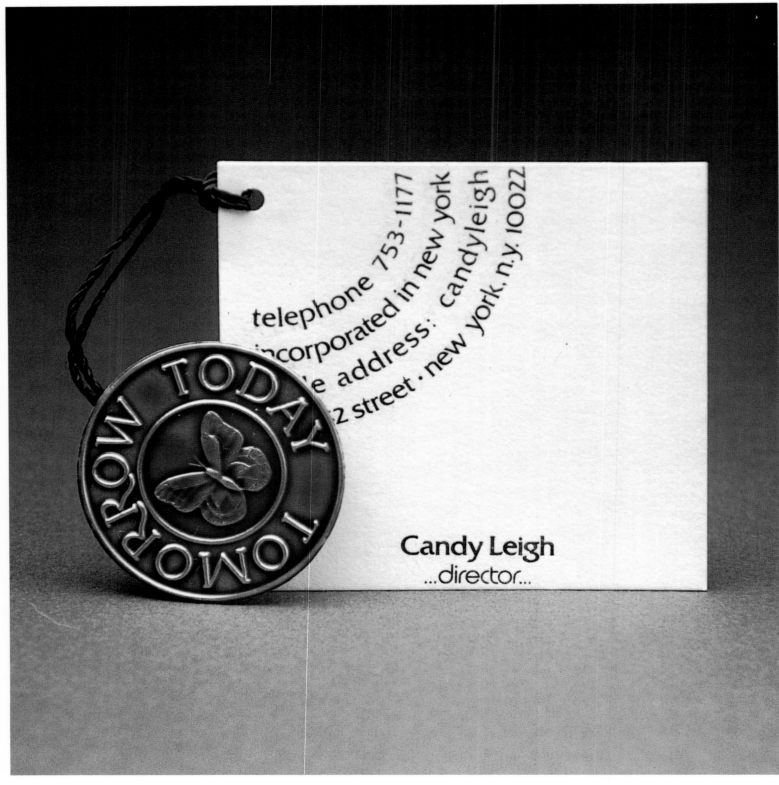

telephone 753-1177
incorporated in new york
le address: candyleigh
2 street · new york. n.y. 10022

Candy Leigh
...director...

CLIENT
Tomorrow Today
DESIGNER
Ely Besalel
LLUSTRATOR
Ely Besalel

CLIENT
Elizabeth Resnick Design
DESIGNER
Elizabeth Resnick
DESIGN FIRM
Elizabeth Resnick Design
PRINTER
Artcraft, Inc.
TYPESETTER
Don Dewsnap Typographic Services
DESIGN AWARDS
**Typography 12—Type Directors
Club Award**

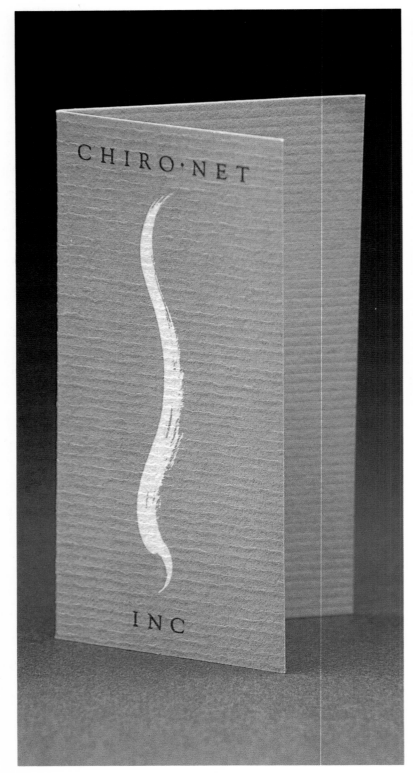

DR. SCOTT D. PROWELL

Provider Liaison

222 W. Gregory Suite 110
Kansas City, MO 64114
(816) 333-1118

CLIENT
Chiro Net, Inc.
DESIGNER
Patrice Eilts
DESIGN FIRM
Eilts, Anderson & Tracy Design
MANUFACTURER
Insty Prints
TYPESETTER
Deidre Eilts
ILLUSTRATOR
Patrice Eilts
Bill Ray
DESIGN AWARDS
PIE *Business Stationery*
Letterhead & Logo Design
Gold—Kansas City Art Directors

CLIENT
Huck's Landing, Inc.
Thomas D. Carter
DESIGNER
Larry McAdams
DESIGN FIRM
The McAdams Group
ILLUSTRATOR
Larry McAdams
TYPESETTER
Orange County Type
DESIGN AWARDS
OCAF Awards

Huck's Landing, Inc.   23591 El Toro Rd., #190 El Toro, CA 92630

Thomas D. Carter   President   (714) 951-9007

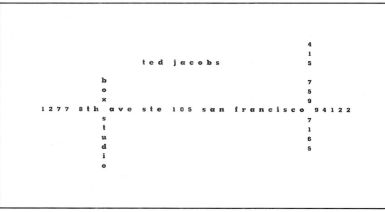

CLIENT
Box Studio
DESIGNER
Ted Jacobs
DESIGN FIRM
Box Studio
TYPESETTER
Box Studio
ILLUSTRATOR
Box Studio

ted jacobs
box studio
1277 8th ave ste 105 san francisco 94122
415 759 7165

BOX STUDIO   SAN FRANCISCO
94122
TED JACOBS
HOPE
1894 11TH AVE
415 759 7165

Appendix

A. Cutler Design
309 West 57 St.
New York, NY 10019

After Dinner Design
537 West Derning Pl. #301
Chicago, IL 60614

Akagi Design
632 Commercial St.
San Francisco, CA 94111

Alan Disparte Design
621 York St.
San Francisco, CA 94110

Antero Ferreira Design
Rua De Roriz
4100 Porto
Portugal

April Greiman Inc.
620 Moulton Ave. #211
Los Angeles, CA 90031

Art Chantry Design
P.O. Box 4069
Seattle, WA 98104

ART F X
8945 Pottawattami
Skokie, IL 60026

Aufuldish & Warinner
304 William Ave.
Larkspur, CA 94939

Barnstorming Designs
11423 Fruitwood Way
Germantown, MD 20876

Box Studio
1894 11th Ave.
San Francisco, CA 94122

Brainstorm Unlimited Inc.
166 Lexington Ave.
New York, NY 10016

Bright & Associates, Inc.
53 Bonn Place
Weehawken, NJ 07087

Brodkin & Associates
RD-1, Box 139 A
Mullica Hill, NJ 08062

Bruce Yelaska Design
1546 Grant Ave.
San Francisco, CA 94133

Calvo Object Design
48 Ninth Ave. #6A
New York, NY 10011

Catherine Vogel Design
52 West Montrose Ave.
South Orange, NJ 07079

Charles S. Anderson Design Co.
30 North First St.
Minneapolis, MN 55401

Chermayeff & Geismar Inc.
15 East 26th St.
12th Floor
New York, NY 10010

Christine McFarren
327 Guerrero St.
San Francisco, CA 94103

Ciro Design
28441 Las Arubas
Laguna Niguel, CA 92656

Clifford Selbert Design
2067 Massachusetts Ave.
Cambridge, MA 02140

Clockwork Apple Inc.
St. Laight St.
New York, NY 10013

Coblyn Design
5020 Malden Dr.
Bethesda, MD 20816

Cordella Design
855 Boylston St.
Boston, MA 02116-2601

COY Los Angeles
9520 Jefferson Blvd.
Culver City, CA 90232

Crosby Associates Inc.
676 North St. Clair St.
Room 1805
Chicago, IL 60611

Cullinare Design Inc.
260 Fifth Ave.
New York, NY 10001

D-Zine, Inc.
34 West 15th St.
New York, NY 10011

Daly & Daly Inc.
233 Harvard St.
Brookline, MA 02146

David Morris Design Associates
66 York St.
Jersey City, NJ 07302

Davie and Lindholm Design
Partnership
182 Willard St.
New Haven, CT 06515-2030

Dennard Creative Inc.
13601 Preston Rd.
Suite 814
Carillon Tower East
Dallas, Texas 75240

design M design W
22 Second St.
Troy, NY 12180

Design Matters
330 East 38th St.
New York, NY 10016

Design Partnership/Portland
500 NW Ninth Ave.
Portland, OR 97209

Design Squad
18 East 16th Street
New York, NY 10003

Designsense
10 Exchange St.
P.O. Box 7829
Portland, ME 04112

Designwerks!
1642 Las Tratipas
Alamo, CA 94507

Direct Design
7 Kilburn St.
Burlington, VT 05401

DMZ
477 Pacific Ave.
San Francisco, CA 94133

Downing & Filzow Graphic Design
400 Washington St.
Suite LL3
Braintree, MA 02184-4729

Earl Gee Design
501 Second St.
Suite 700
San Francisco, CA 94107

Edwin Schlossberg Incorporated
641 Sixth Ave.
New York, NY 10011

Eilts, Anderson & Tracy Design
2806 West 49th Terr
Shawnee Mission, KS 66205

Elizabeth Resnick Grpahic Design
126 Payson Rd.
Chestnut Hill, MA 02167

Emily Ruth Cohen
Graphic Design Business Consultant
14 Hurley Ave.
North Plainfield, NJ 07060

Eric Baker Design Associates, Inc.
156 Fifth Ave. #508
New York, NY 10010

Eymer Design
25 Dry Dock Ave.
Boston, MA 02210

Fani Chung Design
501 Second St.
San Francisco, CA 94107

Frank Renile
500 Aurora Ave. North
Seattle, WA 98109

Full Circle Graphics
17 J Princes Rd.
Lawrenceville, NJ 08648

Gamble Design
9 Sheafe St.
Portsmouth, NH 03801

GVO, Inc.
2470 Embarcadero Way
Palo Alto, CA 94303

Harrison Design Group
665 Chestnut
San Francisco, CA 94133-2305

Higashi Glaser Design
122 West 20th St.
New York, NY 10011

Hula Lei
40-18 215 Place
Bayside, NY 11361

Identity Design
109 Spring St.
Newport, RI 02840

Information Graphics
257 West 21st St.
New York, NY 10011

Iris Bell
333 East 49th St.
Apt. 4L
New York, NY 10017

J. Graham Hanson
817 Second Ave. #3
New York, NY 10017

Jacek Przybyszewski
9 East 17 St.
New York, NY 10003

Jack Lowry Design
1942 Leavenworth St.
San Francisco, CA 94133

Jack Rizzo Computer Aided Design
26 Kinney St.
Madison, NJ 07940

Jack Tom Design
80 Varick St.
Suite 3-B
New York, NY 10013

James L. Selak Design
5 Beatrice Cove
Fairport, NY 14450

Jann Church Partners Advertising &
Graphic Design
110 Newport Center Dr.
Suite 160
Newport Beach, CA 92660

Jeff Johnson
63-B Maverick Square #11
East Boston, MA 02128

João Machado
Rua Padre Xavier Couthinho, 125
4100 Porto
Portugal

JOED Design
445 West Erie
Chicago, IL 60610

John Kneapler
48 West 21st St.
12th Floor
New York, NY 10010

John Korinko Design
1403 Rt. 23
Butler, NJ 07405

Judi Radice Design Consultant
(JRDC)
P.O. Box 26710
San Francisco, CA 94126

Kan Tai-Keung Design & Associates
Ltd.
28/F Washington Plaza
230 Wanchai Rd.
Hong Kong

Karen Guancione Art & Design
262 De Witt Ave.
Belleville, NJ 07109

Katharine Nemec
4 Peter Cooper Rd.
Apt. 9B
New York, NY 10010

Keller In Print
1747 Westchester Pike #24
Havertown, PA 19083

Lam & Company
130 West 25th St.
New York, NY 10001

Larry Vigon Studio
5818 West Third St.
Los Angeles, CA 90036

Lisa Levin Design
2269 Chestnut St.
Suite 436
San Francisco, CA 94123

Lorna Stovall Design
1088 Queen Anne Place
Los Angeles, CA 90019

Louey/Rubino Design Group Inc.
2525 Main St.
Suite 204
Santa Monica, CA 90405

M plus M Incorporated
17 Cornelia St.
New York, NY 10014

Machineart
66 Willow Ave.
Hoboken, NJ 07030

Manville Bakacs Santana Inc.
95 Horatio St. #203
New York, NY 10014

Marc English Design
57 Exeter St.
Arlington, MA 02174

Marie Sterte
Skardalsliden 1
44536 Bohus
Sweden

Mark Oldach Design
2138 West Haddon
Chicago, IL 60622

Marsha Drebelbis Studio
Brookriver Center
Suite 208
South 8150 Brookriver Dr.
Dallas, TX 75247

Martine Bruel Design
77 Martin St.
Cambridge, MA 02138

Michael Salisbury Communications
2200 Amapola Court
Torrance, CA 90501

Michael Stanard, Inc.
1000 Main St.
Evanston, IL 60202

Miggs B Design
Box 6
Westport, CT 06881

Mike Armijo Design Office
3131 West 180th Place
Torrnance, CA 90504

Mike Quon Design Office Inc.
568 Broadway
New York, NY 10012

Milton Glaser Inc.
East 32nd St.
New York, NY 10016

Morla Design
463 Bryant St.
San Francisco, CA 94107

No Dogs Design
28 Eliot St.
Boston, MA 02130

Notovitz Design, Inc.
47 East 19th St.
New York, NY 10003

On Call/Candice Swanson
1609 Holt St.
Ft. Worth, TX 76103

Ostro Design
147 Fern St.
Hartford, CT 06105

Patricia Curtan Design & Printing
1544 Blake St.
Berkeley, CA 94703

Patrick Soohoo Designers
8800 Venice Blvd.
Suite A
Los Angeles, CA 90034

Pentagram Design Limited
11 Needham Rd.
London W112RP
England

Peter Lord
206 East 17th St. #6A
New York, NY 10003-3636

Pisarkiewicz & Co. Inc.
34 West 22nd St.
New York, NY 10010

Platinum Design
14 West 23rd St.
New York, NY 10010

plus design, inc.
10 Thatcher St.
Suite 109
Boston, MA 02113

Pod Design
318 East Hadley Ave.
Dayton, OH 45419

Pollard Design
RR1 Box 274
East Hartland, CT 06027

Praxis Design & Consultant
Suite 200
1200 West Pender St.
Vancouver

Profile Design
151 Townsend St.
San Francisco, CA 94107

Quinn Brei Design
1919 North Oakland
Milwaukee, WI 53202

Red Square Design
150 West 11 St.
New York, NY 10011

Reliable Design Studios, Inc.
611 Broadway
Room 742
New York, NY 10012

Rick Eiber Design (RED)
4649 Sunnyside North
Seattle, WA 98103

Rigelhaupt Design
18 East 16th St.
4th Floor
New York, NY 10003

Robin Ghelerter Illustration &
Design
1118 South Sherbourne #1
Los Angeles, CA 90035

Rochelle Seltzer Design
30 The Fenway
Boston, MA 02215

Rod Dyer Group, Inc. Design &
Advertising
8360 Melrose Ave.
3rd Floor
Los Angeles, CA 90069

Romeo Empire Design
154 Spring St.
3rd Floor
New York, NY 10012

Ross Design Inc.
2132 North Market St.
Wilmington, DE 19802

Roth + Associates
103 Cornelia St.
Boonton, NJ 07005

Ruby Shoes Studio
124 Watertown St.
Suite 1E
Watertown, MA 02177

Sagoma Design Group
P.O. Box 2757
Kennebunkport, ME 04046

Salestrom Design, Inc.
434 Sixth Ave.
New York, NY 10011

Samenwerkende Ontwerpers bv
Design Consultancy
Herengracht 160
1016 BN Amsterdam
The Netherlands

Sayles Graphic Design
308 Eighth Street
Des Moines, IA 50309

Sean Adams
2130 Lync Ave.
Los Angeles, CA 90027

Sean Michael Edwards Design, Inc.
28 West 25th St.
5th Floor
New York, NY 10010

Seymour Robins Design
1690 Boardman St.
Sheffield, MA 01257

Shelley Danysh Studio
8940 Krewstown Rd. #107
Philadelphia, PA 19115

Smart Design Inc.
7 West 18th St.
New York, NY 10011

Sommese Design
481 Glenn Rd.
State College
Pennsylvania 16801

Sonsoles Llorens
Pg. de Sant Joan 36 pral. 10
08010 Barcelona

Spot Design
775 Sixth Ave.
6th Floor
New York, NY 10001

Stark Design Associates
22 West 19th St.
9th Floor
New York, NY 10011

Index

Clients

Designers